FOREWO

Well, another year over and I'm happy to report
catastrophes as far as the society is concerned, quite
members and others providing an excellent program
subscribed, with standing room only at some sinc
Ticket Tailor.

The publications department is undergoing some changes. A while ago it was decided to reproduce the Jeremiah Cruse map of 1813 as a full-scale atlas and the number of presales surpassed our expectations as has interest in the project in general. It has now been published and available from the museum in a limited and numbered edition of 500 copies.

We are also exploring the possibility of establishing a register of 'Members Interests' or a database of historical projects bringing together past research and tasks for the future in an easily accessible format. Further details will appear in *Contact* as progress is made. Another idea is a serious updating of Rodney Goodall's best-selling *Buildings of Frome*.

Frome Society Publications On-Line

Since its formation in 1958 our society has produced approaching 100 books pamphlets and publications on the history of the town and its surrounding villages. The majority of these have been out of print for many years and often the only copy is to be found in the museum library. Increasing printing costs and problems with distribution mean that reprinting the majority of them is no longer viable.

To avoid many decades of research being lost we have worked in collaboration with Frome Museum to produce copies in PDF format and made them available free of charge on their website. Titles include some important items from other publishers and they can be found on the museum website (www.frome-heritage-museum.org) under *Search Our Collection* type in the book title and click on the *Digital Links* at the bottom. The download can take several minutes as some of the items are quite large.

The Frome Yearbook first published in 1987 and has now reached its 26th volume. Back issues are available in PDF format free of charge. A complete list of the contents of each volume is available from publications@fsls.org.

Mick Davis. Editor.

In Memorandum

A watercolour of the ancient manor house of the Champneys of Orchardleigh in July 1859 shortly before demolition. Parts of the house were thought to date back to Tudor times or before and had been in the hands of the family since the mid fifteenth century.

The artist is unknown but possibly Frances Smith a prolific watercolourist and first cousin to Edina Duckworth, the wife of Reverend William Arthur Duckworth who inherited the new house of 1856 from his father William.

I am grateful to Martin Shepherd for this information.

The original is in Frome Museum

ROSE RACHEL POCOCK 1810-1879

Frome's Forgotten Artist

Mick Davis

M⁺ GEORGE POCOCK,

BRISTOL

Rachel Rose Pocock was born on 30 May 1810 the daughter of George Pocock (1774-1843) a school master, originally from Hungerford, and his wife Elizabeth Rose who was born in Rode. The pair married at St John's in Frome in 1797 and between them produced an impressive 14 children. Since 1795 they had lived at Westbrook House, now 33 Vicarage Street at the end of Blindhouse Lane which they leased from the Marquis of Bath.[1] The family moved to Bristol in 1800 and George become the proprietor of a private school named the Prospect Place Academy; boarders paid 25 guineas per year and day pupils 4. The school lay just under St. Michael's Church and was entered via a gothic arch made from the jaw bone of a whale.

George became a preacher at the Wesleyan, Portland Chapel in Bristol but remained constantly at war with its leaders producing a number of tracts attacking them over the question of educating the poor. One of his more unorthodox ideas involved preaching from tents which he took around mining camps spreading the word with some success using his practical skills to construct one capable of holding 500 people but his vitriolic attacks proved too much and he was excluded from the movement for some years.

Father George's eccentricities did not end with religion however. In 1827 he produced a book entitled, *The Aeropleustic Art or Navigation of the Air by the Means of Kites or Buoyant Sails,* an outlandish idea which had kites providing the motive power in place of horses. So overpowering was this obsession that he almost sacrificed two of his children to it. His third son Alfred was launched aboard a kite-drawn sledge on Bristol Downs which the wind took 'with a velocity so great that all attempts to overtake it were quite fruitless'. The Downs at that time were pitted with quarries and the future coach to England's greatest cricketer was almost dashed to pieces, nor was his daughter Martha spared, being launched into the sky in a chair attached to huge kite.

Frome philanthropist Thomas Bunn was not impressed with the man and wrote in his diary for 24 August 1844,

> Mr and Mrs Pocock, brother and sister, [Alfred and Rose] called for directions respecting some lithographs they are to prepare for me. Their father, was the most conceited, or one of the most disgustingly conceited beings I ever knew, though he derived a large income from his school, he left a large family, his widow and children, wholly unprovided for. He commenced an insurance on his life but did not continue it.[2]

Luckily for the future of English cricket the family survived intact.

George had an elder brother, John Pocock (1769-1804) curate of St John's in Frome, he took over the lease on Westbrook House when his brother George moved to Bristol and [3] it was his son George a schoolmaster, that Rose Rachel Pocock married at St Michael's in Bristol on 30 June 1835.[4] We know nothing of the young Rose before her marriage at the age of 25 when the couple moved into Westbrook House except that she was baptised in the Methodist Chapel in Portland Street, Kingsdown, Bristol in the name, 'Rachel Rose' She had reversed this by the time of her marriage and was henceforth known as 'Rose Rachel'. In all probability she was educated at home by her schoolmaster father but whoever was responsible produced a remarkable artist. In September of 1837 George and Rose had their first child also named Rose who died at the age of one week and was buried at St. John's. The following year, on 21 August they had another daughter Rose Mary Pocock.

George died of consumption on 8 July 1838 at Ovis Farmhouse, Morwenstow, Cornwall presumably while he was staying there to recover his health. In December of that year it was announced that Mrs Pocock, the widow of George Pocock, together with her unmarried cousin Mary (1802-1882), elder sister to George, were to open a 'ladies school in Frome' the following January at a charge of 30 guineas per annum, exclusive of the professor's charges. By the census of 1841 Rose was aged 31 but gave her age as 25 and Mary was 39 but given as 35 as the census of the year allowed the ages of people over 15 to be rounded down to the nearest multiple of five. Rose was the school mistress and Mary her assistant.

Fairlawn House in 2019

The boarding school was at Fairlawn House, Behind Town now Christchurch Street East. Also at the house are Leanna 11, Sarah 7 Elizabeth 5, Rose 3 all Pococks, 12 other female pupils ranging from 8 to 16 and 3 female servants. What went wrong is not known but on 24 December 1841 after only a couple of years the partnership was dissolved and Rose's place was taken by Grace Walker.[5] It is not known when the school ceased to function but by 1850 the pair had moved to Tapton House in Chesterfield the former home of engineer George Stephenson who died there in August of 1848. The 'educational establishment for young ladies' continued until 1865 when the executors of Stephenson's estate sold the building.

During her time in Frome, Rose produced a remarkable series of drawings or lithographs. The least impressive of these, but perhaps historically the most important was a 'drawing on stone' entitled, *The Old Front of Frome Parish Church.* It depicts a blank, austere looking building in various shades of grey and it is only with difficulty that we recognise it as St. John's church and as with all of her known work it is undated. According to McGarvie,[6] after the cutting of Bath Street in 1811 there was pressure to improve the front of the church and 'modernise' its appearance to bring it in line with the Georgian buildings along the new road. A committee was formed in March 1814 and it was agreed to instruct Jeffry Wyatt then working for Lord Bath at Longleat. He submitted plans for the re-facing of the west front with blocks of ashlar six inches thick and this was done by local builder Joseph Chapman at a cost of £231. It is believed that the original front, much decayed, was not removed but lay behind the new.

The West Front before 1815 a lithograph by Rose Pocock taken from Wyatt's sketch
(FM D4637)

The Old Front of Frome Parish Church

The Ashlar West Front of St. John's 1814-1865 (FM P995)

Wyatt also designed the five arched screen separating the road from the churchyard described by Pevsner as 'pretty' - it is difficult to believe that they are by the same hand. Rev.William Bennett described the re-facing of the West Front as exhibiting 'sad ignorance of the principles of church architecture' and 'utterly incongruous' not only that, but the building was in danger of collapse and the ashlar blocks had done nothing to provide support.[7] 'If by chance', he continues, 'there should be any picture or photograph existing of the previous West Front – which in mercy to the architect it is hoped there is not-let him look at that picture which *was* and then the gratify himself with this second picture which *is*.'[8] Bennett had the front rebuilt by1866 after almost 50 years and it remains to this day, squat, heavy and overbearing, lacking the grace and elegance of the original but then anything is an improvement on 1814.

In the early part of 1843 advertisements for a small album entitled *The Longleat Views* by Mrs RR Pocock began to appear in the press. It seems that individual sheets had been available for a while but the whole work was now to be published by subscription and consist of a folio of 14 sheets 24" x 17" on the best paper, available to subscribers for 21 shillings and non-subscribers for 25 shillings. Produced under the patronage the Marquis of Bath and available from Mr Pocock's Library in Bridge Street, Bath or his Lithographic Establishment in Broad Street, Bristol. Alfred Pocock was Rose's brother, younger by four years and we shall come to his story later.

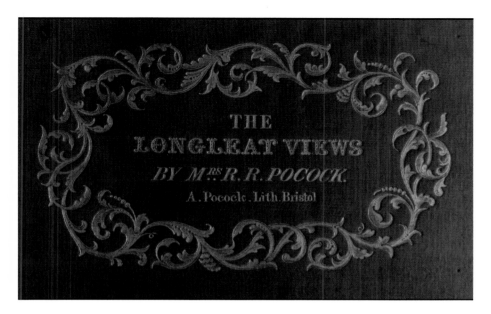

The 1843 Longleat Album by Rose Pocock

The Longleat illustrations were followed in May of 1846 by, *Sketches of Bristol in the Olden Time* another small album of views which portrayed 'several important parts of Bristol with figures in the costume of the reign of Queen Elizabeth' and in September of 1846 advertisements began to appear for a book entitled, '*Aunt Kate's Story; or the Vicar and his Family* by Ann Thorp with four illustrations drawn by Mrs Rose Pocock and lithographed in the first style of the art. To be had of all Booksellers in Bath. Price 2/6d.'

The following year an advertisement appeared in the Bristol papers ;

LITHOGRAPHY, ENGRAVING,
AND PRINTING,
Drawings and Designs, of every description, Railway Maps and Sections, Elevations, Plans, Bill-Heads, Circulars, and Fac-similes, Drawn, Copied, and Printed by ALFRED POCOCK, BROAD-STREET, WINE-STREET, Bristol.

Artists and Amateurs can be supplied with every requisite material for Drawing on Stone, and directions are given to assist young Practitioners.

Mr. POCOCK cannot allow this announcement to appear without expressing his grateful sense of the liberal patronage of many of his late Father's old Pupils (Mr. George Pocock, of Prospect-place Academy) and of the Public.

A Lithographic-Printing APPRENTICE Wanted.

Mr. Pocock's Sister, Mrs. ROSE R. POCOCK, being engaged on several continuous Works of Lithographic Art, has a Vacancy for an ARTICLED PUPIL, either a Lady or a Gentleman.

For Terms apply at Mr. Pocock's Office.

Alfred Pocock was brother to Rose and born in Bristol in 1813. Like his sister his early years are obscure but he was probably educated by his father. He is first mentioned in F.S. Ashley-Cooper's biography of cricketer Edward Mills Grace.[9] 'Strange to say, he did not play cricket until he was twenty-three, but by perseverance ...he became a really good player. Thereafter, he was fanatical!' This would have been 1836 and his fanaticism could not have been put to better use.

Martha Pocock, (1812-1884) sister to Rose and Alfred married a Bristol surgeon named Henry Mills Grace in 1831 and went to live in Downend House, North Street. Henry was an enthusiastic country cricketer and no less than 14 members of the family played at first class level. Two of his sons proved to be outstanding, the first, Edward Mills Grace (1841-1911) was an excellent all-rounder who played in 314 first class matches but it was his younger brother William Gilbert Grace; venerated throughout the world as WG Grace (1848-1915) who became one of England's greatest cricketers dominating 880 first matches including 22 Tests. Both were taught the basics as children by Uncle Alfred an athlete and a natural leader. As a day job Alfred Pocock was a lithographer with his own business at 50 Broad Street, Bristol and it was he that printed and published his sister's works.

In December 1848 Rose married schoolmaster George Mowbray Gilbert at St James Mangotsfield in a ceremony that must have been illegal, as all concerned including the officiant (who will have known the Pocock family well) and the witnesses must surely have known. From the time of the Marriage Act 1835 until 1907, it was illegal to marry one's deceased wife's sister. George had previously been married to Rose's sister Sarah Rose who died in 1847.

By 1851 the now 'Rose Gilbert' and her husband had forsaken Bristol and were running Goodenough House School in Ealing; her last known illustrations were for her eccentric father's, *Treatise on Aeropleustic Art.*

A carriage propelled by kites by R. Gilbert 1851

In the 1860s Alfred expanded his business and produced an excellent advertisement for his new premises still in Broad Street but all was not well and the business went into liquidation in October 1864 and in November 1866 he set sail for Australia and New Zealand playing cricket and making sketches. By the 1871 census he had returned to Bristol, and was back living with the Grace family. He died at Downend, Bristol at the age of 84. Gilbert died in 1877 and Rose in 1879 aged 68.

Alfred Pocock's advertisement for his expanded premises, Bristol, early 1860s

[1] McGarvie *The Book of Frome* p103
[2] Gill *Experiences of a 19th Century Gentleman* p 61
[3] Gill p76
[4] *Bristol Mercury* 30 Jun 1835.
[5] Diary of Thomas Green. Frome Museum
[6] *Light in Selwood* 1976 FSLS
[7] Bennett. *History of the Old Church* 1866 ps 46-48
[8] Bennett p117
[9] FS Ashley-Cooper *Edward Mills Grace.* 1916 p 5

THE FROME POST OFFICE ROBBERY

Nick Stamp

On 3 September 1855 Sarah Watts aged 21 a domestic servant at the Frome Post Office in Vicarage Street was brought up before magistrates Dr Harrison and John Sinkins charged with having stolen a registered letter containing notes and cheques worth over £100, approximately £10,000 in today's money. Accused with her was Charles Druce, 25[1] who was said to have received one of the notes knowing it to have been stolen. Only about £50 had been recovered and the constable in charge, James Nicholls, asked that the two be remanded in custody while he made further enquiries. Satisfied that there was a good case, on 14 September the pair appeared for their summary trial before magistrates, Lord Dungarvan and N. Barton Esq who heard the following evidence.

> The registered packet had contained £101/13/- 18 bank notes and a number of cheques belonging to the Trowbridge Branch of the Wilts and Dorset Bank. The money had been placed in a bag and sealed with sealing wax, before being sent by coach to the Bath Post Office and then on to Frome where it arrived on the morning of 30 August. Opening and checking such bags was the duty of Mary Ann Payne an assistant at the post office who normally came down stairs at about 6.00am to take delivery of the post which normally arrived between 4.30 and 5.00am. On the 30th she found the bags outside the office door, which was locked, and lying on the floor of the passage as usual. The outside door was shut. She carried the bag into the office and noticed that although the seal was unbroken the string seemed to have been tampered with. Opening the packet, she found two registered letters inside and looked for the bill which would give details of what the bag should contain. This was missing. Payne stated that she had noticed that the string on a bag had been cut and re-tied two or three weeks before but as it was so securely tied she thought little of it and had not mentioned it to John Jones the postmaster but now that the letter list was missing she thought she had better report it.

> There was normally a period of about an hour when she would be alone with the bags and nothing had been missed before the arrival of Sarah Watts. Since her employment registered letters had been missing on three occasions.

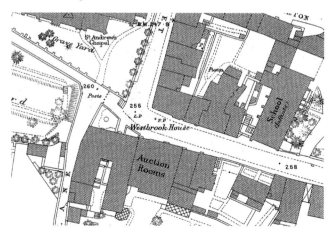

Ordnance Survey Map 1886. In 1855 the Post Office occupied one of the buildings to the left of the school and the Druce family would have been to the right of the Auction Rooms.

Constable James Nicholls gave evidence that on 1 September he accompanied the clerk of the magistrates to the post office, remaining outside while the clerk went in. Whilst there he saw Watts go from her employ to a house directly opposite where the Druce family lived and return almost immediately. Shortly after this he was called into the office and asked to arrest Watts on a charge of having stolen a letter. Watts told him that the 'things' were over the road at Druce's, Nicholls crossed the road and saw Mrs Druce senior who took him upstairs and showed him a box belonging to the prisoner which he took over to the post office. The box was locked and Watts claimed that Mrs Druce had the key but as it was not forthcoming Nicholls broke it open and found six bank notes, a quantity of cash, some jewellery, and various other 'important articles'.

The old Frome Post Office building on the left before demolition in the 1960s, now a car park

James Gough of Stuckey's Bank in Frome gave evidence that Watts had come to the bank on 31 August and presented a cheque for £9/14/- which he cashed for her. He did not find this unusual as her knew her to be employed by the post office and she often cashed cheques for Mr Jones. Watts claimed that she had been shopping in town with Amelia Druce and had given her the remaining notes to look after and that if any were missing she must know about them. When being conveyed to the lock up next to the Blue Boar she said that she would tell all about it if she could be forgiven, a pretty forlorn hope given the amount of money involved and the fact that it was pretty obvious what she had been doing – or perhaps the 'it' she was referring to was a far more serious matter that had occurred some years before.

His suspect safely secured, Nicholls carried out a further search of the Druce house finding various newly bought items including an accordion, a small work box, two new shawls and two new bibles. Amongst the haul were '...earrings which I produce, which, were taken out of Amelia Druce's ears, and given up to me on my asking her for the earrings which were bought by the prisoner in her presence, at Mr Wells, a jeweller, in Cheap St.' The bedroom of Amelia's parents and an attic was also searched finding more goods including three new bonnets, a child's hat and a quantity of new drapery. A search of Watt's bedroom at the post office produced some 'wearing apparel' gold ear drops, and four brooches.

Arthur Hillman, the mail coach driver, gave evidence to say that he had been asked by Watts to tap on the window of the house opposite with his whip when he had delivered the early morning mail. He had done this a number of times at her request and received a response from a man or woman calling out, *Hollo! All right?*. The window in question was pointed out as the bedroom window of Mr and Mrs Druce, the parents of Amelia. When asked about this they claimed that upon this signal they called Amelia, a dress maker, who was having dresses delivered. Mrs Druce also admitted going shopping with Watts and being bought a gold ring and a shawl.

Charlotte Short, who worked in the shop of Mr May a draper in the town knew Watts and remembers her coming into the shop and buying a quantity of fabric with a five-pound note, and on previous occasions she had made purchases accompanied by Amelia Druce.

Susanna Joyce wife of Henry the landlord of the Waggon & Horses in Gentle Street gave evidence that Charles Druce came into the pub on 31 August and had three glasses of whiskey paid for with a five-pound note. Nicholls went looking for Druce but he gave himself up voluntarily saying that he had 'picked the note up'. Further evidence was given of Druce drinking at The Angel run by Henry Harris and getting so tipsy that he slept there. There was little that could be said in their defence. For Druce, it was claimed that he was consistent in his story of having picked up the note, though this was hardly true as he had told Mrs Joyce that he had been left some money by one of his wife's friends and was thinking of going into business.

Vicarage Street in 2000. The Druce family would have occupied one of the houses on the left

Mr Dunn, for Watts, said that she had 'yielded to temptation improperly put in her way by the very negligent conduct of her master.' It was, of course, no excuse but there might be some truth in it as it seems that nothing was done about the registered letters missing on the previous three occasions since Watts had been employed. If postmaster Jones himself was negligent then surely assistant Payne would see it as her duty to report it, unless small gifts were coming her way as well. As for the rest of the Druce family, there would seem to be plenty of evidence for an aiding and abetting charge, or receiving stolen goods, but the police seemed content with the two they had. Sarah Watts, originally from Corsley, had been working as a house servant on a farm in Marston during the 1851 census before being employed at the post office in December 1854, in what must have been a step up the social ladder to a position of trust. It is very sad that she chose to abuse it. The prison description book describes her as 'aged 22 height 5'1½" fair complexion with grey eyes and brown hair, single, cut on the forefinger of her left hand a mole under her left eye and one on her left shoulder'. Druce had a profession and a young family but again, the temptation for easy money proved too much. He was described as 'aged 25, height 5' 6 ¾" sallow complexion, black hair, hazel eyes, married, scar on left cheek, scar on top lip, slightly pockpitted, scar on left thumb'.

The magistrates were satisfied that there was enough for the pair to stand trial at the higher court and they were remanded in custody at Shepton Mallet to await trial at Winter Assizes on 3 December in Taunton. Watts was refused bail and remanded in custody while Druce was granted bail in the sum of £100 himself, with two sureties of £50 but was unable to raise that sum. At Taunton after a brief repetition of the facts and evidence from the various witnesses, they were each found guilty, sentenced to transportation for 14 years and taken to Taunton jail. During this period transportation to Australia was uncommon and sentences were often served on the prison hulks or more likely commuted to prison terms in the UK and this was the case with Watts and Druce. On 2 October 1860 Watts was moved to Burlington Lane Women's Prison, Fulham otherwise known as the Fulham Refuge.

The mention of the Refuge throws an interesting light on the workings of the women's prison system at this time. In 1853 Burlington House and grounds, then in use as a school, were purchased by the government for the purpose of erecting a reformatory home for young female prisoners, the most hopeful cases were selected from the prisons with the hope that they could be permanently 'reclaimed'. The young women were trained in laundry and other industrial occupations, and spent, the last two or three years of the terms of their sentence. After a while the Refuge was turned into an ordinary convict prison, being enlarged to take about 400 prisoners. During its time it had housed another local girl, Constance Kent who in 1877 was moved from Millbank Prison to cell 29, serving 21 years for the murder of her half-brother, Francis Saville Kent, at Road, Somerset, on the night of 29-30 June 1860. Fulham was also temporarily home to the brilliant con-women Madam Rachel and Mrs Gordon-Baillie.[2] Fulham Prison was sold for housing in 1893.

§§§

History had not quite finished with Sarah Watts. Six years later *The Somerset and Wiltshire Journal* of 19 October 1861 had a strange tale to tell which concerned the confession by a Joseph Seer to a murder that had happened ten years before.[5]

> On Friday, Supt. Deggan visited the house of several persons who had lived at the Woodlands in 1851, but from none of them could he obtain any information as to their having any personal knowledge of the prisoner. It has been a kind of tradition in the town that a convict named Sarah Watts, found guilty in 1855 of robbing the Frome Post Office, offered to "tell all about the Woodlands murder if she were let free" This statement has been much talked of since Seer's extra-ordinary confession; and by the direction of the magistrates Supt. Deggan proceeded to

London on Monday with a view of enquiring off Sarah Watts if she knew anything of the prisoner. On his arrival at the Millbank Prison, he found that she had left there for an institution in Brixton and at Brixton he was informed that she was at a refuge at Fulham.

At Fulham he had an interview with her, but she declared she never made the statement attributed to her and denied having any knowledge of the prisoner Joseph Seer, whom she said she had never seen, nor even heard of. In the course of the interview the Superintendent found that she was cognizant of the details of the murder, and she suspected one of the three mentioned in 1851 of being the murderer. Being at the time in service near the spot, it was natural she should have a lively remembrance of all the circumstances of the tragedy. On account of her good conduct she is to be discharged in December next.

In 1851 a young girl of 14 was raped and murdered at Battle Farm at West Woodlands on the outskirts of Frome, the victim's name was Sarah Watts and the murder is unsolved to this day. [3]Our Sarah Watts was in service at a farm in Marston very near the murder site and her knowledge of the attack would have come from being party to local gossip - presumably amplified by having the same name as the victim. Four local men were charged with the murder but acquitted and there the matter seemed to end until ten years had passed and Superintendent Deggan received a visit from a strange young man, an ex-sailor named Joseph Seer who confessed to having murdered Sarah Watts ten years before. Careful investigation seemed to reveal that he was not only mentally unstable but out of the country at the time, but there were many uncertainties and differing accounts. However, coincidence did not end there. The maiden name of Watts's shopping friend, Amelia Druce was Seer and she was elder sister to Joseph!

If Joseph Seer had murdered Sarah Watts could he have confided in his big sister Amelia who then told her best friend Sarah– in the strictest confidence of course – but when faced with an accusation of stealing the equivalent of £10,000 any possible avenue of escape is better than none and perhaps she did think that she knew enough to buy her way out. There would have been no point in repeating her story to Deggan when she was so close to release and a stirring up bad memories all over again.

Amelia Druce and nine-year-old Sarah were admitted to the Union Workhouse, Christchurch Street, Frome on 28 May 1858[4] and she had a second child shortly after, Albert, born on 1 July 1858 presumably out of wedlock as Charles would have still been in Millbank Prison, his wife and child left destitute. The family was still in the workhouse for the census of 7 April 1861 and Amelia died on 7 March 1866 in Swindon, the death certificate showing her to be wife of Charles a factory labourer. We can guess here that when Charles was released from prison he collected his wife and children and moved away to Swindon. He married twice more before moving to Battersea and dying aged 54 in 1885, a boiler maker's assistant.

[1] Charles Druce baptized 30 October 1828 at Badcox Baptist Chapel
[2] *The Adventures of a Victorian Con Woman.* Mick Davis & David Lassman. Pen & Sword 2020
[3] *Frome Times* 2 October 1861
[4] Druce Ancestry website
[5] The full story of the murder and its aftermath is told in the book, *'The Awful Killing of Sarah Watts'* by Mick Davis & David Lassman. Pen & Sword 2018

FOSSILS FROM A BADGER SETT

Simon Carpenter

When I was in my early twenties (I'm now in my mid-60s) I made regular evening visits to watch badgers at a sett on the edge of Saltford between Bristol and Bath where I was living before moving to Frome. It was during one of these trips that I picked up a small lump of fossil-rich clay containing a profusion of small fish scales and teeth (this is described as a 'bone bed' because of the high concentration of disassociated bones it contains). These bones were identified as coming from fish and marine reptiles whose remains accumulated on the sea floor during the final stage of the Triassic Period, (205.5–201 million years ago).

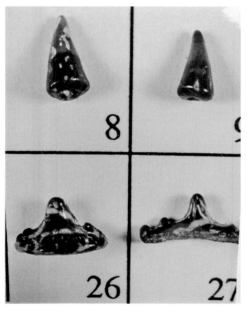

The bone bed is usually interpreted as having been deposited by storm activity in a marine environment during the final phase of the Triassic Period. In the area around Bristol, at that time, the landscape comprised a topography of eroded carboniferous limestone, forming hills and lowlands (much as it does today). The Late Triassic sea flooded over much of the lower-lying areas, depositing bone beds as it went. As sea levels rose, the Mesozoic sediments accumulated around the shorelines, leaving the carboniferous hills as islands in a new archipelago, lying at the time in tropical latitudes.

A selection of Late Triassic fish teeth from Saltford (all less than 1mm in size).

Photo: Simon Carpenter

The lump had been expelled by the badgers during their excavations and was lying on the surface of the spoil. I was feeling particularly lucky and pleased with myself. The lump could easily have been missed, but now I had it in my hand and could see a number of small glass-like pointed teeth protruding from its surface. As the evening light was failing, I decided to return the following day to see if I could find more.

The sett occupies a large area on a wooded slope and has been occupied by badgers for over a century or more and remains active to this day. Although a thorough search was made of the spoil no additional material was found and it would take several more months before, almost by accident, I noticed a layer of clay containing teeth, well below the surface, but close enough to reach with my arm at full stretch down the badger hole.

Over the following few years I extracted enough clay to sieve, using my mother's old tights for this purpose. The rich residue of small teeth, scales and bones (see picture) was later identified by fossil fish expert, Dr. Chris Duffin.

Professor Mike Benton examining the fossil-rich clay with Dr. Chris Duffin looking on.

Photo. Simon Carpenter

Many years passed and in late 2017, I revisited the site to relocate the fossil-rich layer. The badgers in the interim years had completely re-engineered the surface and many of the large elm trees I had used to fix the location had been felled. It took several determined visits before the layer was found again. I thought the site and the fossils would make an exciting project for Bristol University, Earth Sciences Department. My offer was taken up by Professor Mike Benton and in 2018, accompanied by some of his students (see picture) and Dr Chris Duffin, a section was carefully dug through the bone bed layer, so as not to disturb the badgers. A sieving project was set up at Bristol University and a student, Matthieu Moreau assigned to write it all up. The research has been published in the *Proceedings of the Geologists' Association* and is one of a series of similar papers describing Late Triassic bone beds in the South West – all coordinated by Professor Benton.

I am very grateful for all the professional help offered by Bristol University. It has been particularly satisfying to see this fossil-rich site receive the attention it deserves. Nick Mould, Deputy Land Steward, Duchy of Cornwall is thanked for allowing the excavation to proceed. I must also thank the badgers, because without their superior digging abilities, I would never have tripped over the fossils in the first place.

The paper has been published in the *Proceedings of the Geologists' Association* and can be found here:

Matthieu Moreau, Christopher J. Duffin, Claudia Hildebrandt, Deborah Hutchinson, Adam Parker, Simon Carpenter, Michael J. Benton. 2021 Microvertebrates from the Rhaetian basal bone bed of Saltford, near Bath, SW England. Proceedings of the Geologists' Association Volume 132, Issue 2 Pages 147-252.

THE HUNDRED OF FROME

Dr John Harvey

This article has been adapted from a pamphlet originally produced by the Frome Historical Research Group in 1978.

Hundred, Parish & Tithing

 It is believed that King Alfred divided the Kingdom of Wessex into shires or counties, and each county into hundreds during the ninth century. Somerset had 40 hundreds, the largest number of any county in Wessex. In theory each hundred consisted of 100 families of freemen each supported upon a hide of land which consisted of about 120 acres excluding additional areas of meadow, woodland and wasteland over which there were rights of grazing and the like. Ten families, needing ten hides made up a tithing, sometimes identical with a whole parish. In the larger parishes there might be several tithings, in Frome itself there were three. Local government in Saxon Wessex was based the association of responsible householders – the heads of the families, in groups of ten. This formed a system of mutual security called *'frankpledge'*, the members of each tything standing surety for each other and having a communal responsibility for the maintenance of law and order. In course of time the local burden of maintaining roads and bridges also became associated with the frankpledge. This system at first comprised only free (frank) men; but villeins (who were bound to perform labour services for their manorial lord in respect of their lands), had been incorporated into the system by the thirteenth century. By that time local government operated on three levels: the county, the hundred, and the manor. For each of these there were regular courts, those for the county held under the sheriff, initially, twice a year. The 'View of Frankpledge' which all men were bound to attend was after 1217 held only once yearly at Michaelmas. This 'sheriff's tourn' as it was known, was held for the two hundreds of Frome and Kilmersdon, at 'Madbarrow', a long barrow on Buckland Down, also known as Big Tree but now destroyed.[1]

The site of 'Big Tree' Barrow in 2015

17

The lords of individual manors were often granted the right of holding the 'view' in the manor itself, so that the householders did not have to travel to the meeting place of the hundred, and officers including the important constable, were elected locally. This right constituted what became known as the Court Leet which had jurisdiction over the inspection of bread and ale along with many petty offences which were gradually transferred to the Justices of the Peace. In the case of less important manors the annual appointment of officers was made in the court of the hundred which met every three weeks but only two (later one) full courts were held to deal with matters of frankpledge.

Local government, on the same fundamental lines, lasted from the ninth century to the nineteenth; the last of its substantial duties was its liability to make good damages caused by rioters which was removed by an act in 1886. The hundred still survives, following the example of earlier histories of counties. The modern Victoria County Histories and the county volumes of the English Place Name Society deal with parishes in the hundreds to which they belong. Meanwhile the modern division into rural and urban districts began in 1872 and was fully established by 1894. This was superseded by new districts in 1974. It is noteworthy that there has been a steady increase in size from the hundreds to the rural districts and again to the new districts; local government becoming progressively more remote from the individual.

Originally the lord of each hundred was the king who exercised authority through the sheriff. It is a matter of interest that whereas the English High Sheriff has become essentially a non-functional, the sheriff of a county in the states of the Northern American Union is still responsible for law and order. During the middle ages the lordship of many hundreds was granted away by the crown, and in the private hundreds so created the courts were held by the lord's steward instead of the king's sheriff. The hundred as well as the town of Frome was granted by Henry I to the de Courseulles, from whom, by the thirteenth century, it had come to the family of Branch. This is why the principal manor in the parish has long been known as Frome Branch, (also known as Frome Vallis). Subordinate manors were formed and in one case a very large area split off before 1086 forms the endowment of the parish church; the glebe or rectorial manor, assigned later to Cirencester Abbey. After the dissolution this became the manor of West Woodlands. The eastern part of Frome Branch (beyond West Woodlands), was still later sold and became the estate reputed as 'the Manor of East Woodlands'. The lords of Frome West Woodlands held the View of Frankpledge as shown by surviving court rolls of 1568-69 held by the John Rylands Library in Manchester.

Boundaries

The boundaries of early parishes and manors were very slow to change and as a general rule it may be stated that they remained constant from Saxon times until after 1840. The parish was an area from which the tithes (tenth part of the produce), were set aside to provide the endowment (benefice) of a church. Hence the precise area from which tithes were collected was basic knowledge for every incoming parson of a church, and also well known to all inhabitants that disputes were seldom possible. The only exception was in regard to common rights or areas of wasteland between parishes. As an outcome of the Tithe Act of 1836 maps on a very large scale were surveyed for almost every parish so that an almost complete record of all the ancient boundaries survives. It is these old boundaries that are marked on the map below. The boundaries of the three tithings in Frome are also derived from the Tithe Map, and can be found as well in the plan of John Ladd from 1744.[2]

The Liberties.

The lords of certain manors, often religious houses, were granted special privileges including exemption from the duty of attendance at the hundred courts. Such exempt manors were termed Liberties, but as time went on they tended to be reckoned in with an adjacent hundred for certain purposes. In this way three liberties became loosely attached to the hundred of Frome: Mells and Leigh, which had belonged to Glastonbury Abbey; Witham 'Friary', (really Frary from the French *frerie* the lay brotherhood) the precinct given to Hugh of Avalon for the Carthusian order in 1179; and East Cranmore, though in the Middle Ages this last had belonged to the remote hundred of Bempstone. Witham, besides being a liberty, was also an ecclesiastical Peculiar exempt from jurisdiction of the Bishop and Archdeacon and with its own court of probate for wills and administrations.

Miscellaneous notes

The scale of the map is too small to show the many isolated parcels of land which belonged to one parish although situated within another. Larger detached areas are marked belonging to Marston Bigot and to Elm. Outside of the hundred a detached part of the Wiltshire parish of Norton Bavant is marked to the south of Corsley. The precinct of Brewham Lodge, south of Witham was not part of the parish system and became attached for administrative purposes to the much smaller extra-parochial area Eastrip between Bruton and South Brewham. Chatley was a small extra-parochial area in the parish of Woolverton. Rodden, though eventually a Somerset parish was originally a chapelry belonging to the distant parish of Boyton in Wiltshire.

The tithing of Yarnfield, in Somerset, formed part of the Wiltshire parish of Maiden Bradley; similarly, the Somerset tithing of Gasper belonged to Stourton parish in Wiltshire. Buckland Dinham north of Great Elm, (and in modern times united with it as a joint benefice) was a Peculiar attached to a prebend (the same word as provender) is that part of the total revenue of a collegiate church granted to one of the canons for his support; also used of the estate from which it is drawn, in Wells Cathedral.

Standerwick, though long since united with Beckington, retained its separate identity for some official purposes. On the other hand, Fairoak in Berkeley (without known boundaries) represents the lost mediaeval parish of Egforton and another lost parish or chapelry, Pikewell, was absorbed into Frome; it was probably the excrescence north of the river and the south of Orchardleigh. Whitbourne in Corsley was an estate with its own chapel belonging to the order of Templars, (later to be the Hospitallers of St. John) and was administered by the Preceptory of Templecombe. Another possession of the Hospitallers was the scattered manor of Newbury, in Babington parish, partly in the hundred of Frome but in small parcels not all of which have been identified.

It should be noted that the northern part of the boundary between Rode and Woolverton as shown on the map, is a simplification of the very complex situation shown on the joint Tithe Map for the two parishes.

Churches

The map marks the positions of the ancient parish churches with a + so far as they are known, and of a few early chapels of ease such as those at Chesterblade in Evercreech, Wyke Champflower in Bruton, Whitbourne in Corsley and Dilton in Westbury.

Hamlets and minor place names.

Many parishes in addition to a main nucleus at or near the church, had subsidiary settlements. In Frome itself there were, Clink, Keyford, and Vallis, (marked on the map) and more besides such as Feltham and Tytherington. Other examples are Peart in Laverton; Rudge in Beckington; Vobster in Mells; Leighton in Cloford and Trudoxhill in Nunney. In the case of Oldford in Berkeley parish there are small parts of the parishes or manors of Beckington, Frome, Laverton, Lullington, Rodden and Standerwick inextricably mixed, on a scale too small to show on this map. Outside of the hundred are Southwick in North Bradley; Chapmanslade on the boundaries of three parishes, Corsley, Dilton, and Upton Scudamore: Zeals in Mere; Redlynch in Bruton; Coleford in Kilmersdon; Faulkland in Hemington and Shoscombe in Wellow. A few other places are marked, mostly manors or reputed manors, such as Flintford in Frome and Bremeridge in Dilton, with the great houses of Longleat on the borders of Longbridge Deverill and Horningsham, Stourhead in Stourton and Ammerdown in Kilmersdon.

Selwood Forest.

Independent of the boundaries of hundreds, parishes and tithings were the bounds of Selwood Forest, a legal entity subject to the forest law. As the word indicates (forest is the same as foreign i.e. external) the forest was outside the ordinary jurisdictions and the common law. Selwood Forest in Wiltshire extended over the whole of the part of that county shown on the map and northwards up to the River Avon; in Somerset at an early date it went as far south as Penselwood and Stoke Trister, westward to take in Charlton Musgrove, the eastern parts of Shepton Montague and Bruton; Upton Noble, half of Wanstrow, part of Cloford, up to Rodden. By the thirteenth century a large part of this area had been disafforested and the precise course of the new boundaries has been traced. [3]

Natural Features

The ancient county boundary between Somerset and Wiltshire lies in part along an escarpment of high ground rising past Gare Hill to Alfred's Tower, (built 1766-72), a mile south of the further boundary of Witham. Further north the line is an arbitrary one, cutting off the upper waters of several tributaries of the River Frome and at Rode reaching the river which then becomes the boundary. The limits of the hundred follow the course of streams westward and cut across country leaving out Hemington, Hardington, and Buckland Dinham, which physically form part of the area. On the south-west Wanstrow stretches as far as that watershed between the basins of the Nunney Brook and the Alham, while Witham includes the upper waters of the Frome. The parish of Corsley almost exactly corresponds with the other valleys of the Rodden Brook and the Whitbourne and its bounds lie mostly along the summits of the surrounding ridges. Corsley and its outlier Chapmanslade, form a natural extension of the Frome district and have sociologically been linked with Somerset rather than Wiltshire.

THE HUNDRED OF FROME AND ADJACENT PARISHES

ANCIENT BOUNDARIES

FROME SOCIETY FOR LOCAL STUDY : HISTORICAL RESEARCH GROUP

J.H.H. 1978

[1] John Strachey, *History of Somerset.* Mick Davis, *Of Mounds & Men.*

[2] Longleat Muniments 845/50

[3] McGarvie, *The Bounds of Selwood*

21

THE DECLINE & FALL OF VALLIS MANOR

Mick Davis

One of the saddest episodes in Frome's architectural history is the progressive destruction of one of its most ancient buildings. Since its foundation in 1958 the Frome Society for Local Study has made some notable progress in its efforts to record, repair and conserve the town's ancient buildings, some of national importance, but not every attempt has been successful.

The origins and history of Vallis Manor have proved very difficult to trace. Historian Michael McGarvie suggests that it was possible that the original manor was constructed as long ago as the twelfth century as home to Wandrille de Courcelles Lord of the Manor of Frome.[1] On firmer ground he traces its building to 1235 when it was said to have been constructed or perhaps rebuilt out of ten oaks given to a Ralph FitzBernard by King Henry III, about three miles from the town. It is also possible that it began life as a hunting 'box' or lodge on the edge of the flourishing town and the great Forest of Selwood. It is also probable that this is where King Edward I stayed during his visit to Frome on 14 September 1276.

The manor passed to the Leversedge family who were originally from Liversedge in Yorkshire, and became Lords of the Manor through marriage to the then lord's daughter Elizabeth Winslade in the 1390s. A William Leversedge is recorded as having been born there in 1436. There is a famous legend that in 1465 Edmund Leversedge, a proud, argumentative and unpleasant man was struck by a pestilence, possibly the plague, causing his face and tongue to turn as black as pitch and that he lay for a considerable time, (some say 40 days!) as if dead. During this episode, he had the most terrible dream during which he was taken down to Hell and given a guided tour. He awoke, so the legend goes, to find himself laid out for his burial, with his lamenting friends around his bier. The experience terrified him so much that once he recovered he became a reformed man. The Leversedge family embarked upon a major reconstruction of the manor in the fifteenth century and nothing still standing by the early 1970s has been discovered that pre-dates that time. Whatever its origins the manor played a large part in the life of the town and its government during this period.

Disaster struck in 1606 when, as the result of a felony, possibly a murder, committed by Elizabeth Leversedge and three of her servants, the family had to sign away much of their land to obtain a pardon. The situation was not helped when they supported King Charles during the civil war and were twice heavily fined by Parliament. Later generations did not live at Vallis and the house was allowed to deteriorate with the magnificent parkland turned into a farm. One of their family, Lionel Seaman, who became vicar of Frome in 1742, built the vicarage near the church and lived there. The family had sold off parts of the estate over the years and what was left in 1751 was sold to John Boyle, Earl of Cork and Orrery for £15,900 after an occupancy of 11 generations.
John Boyle

The earl seemed delighted with his new purchase and writing from his seat at nearby Marston House 1752 he describes,

..a most delightful situation and vast command, an old house about a mile and a half from my own that employs me in cutting ivy and pruning up old trees and if it rains I have a large antique room to stretch my legs in and a little closet of books within. In the summer I shall probably put up a bit in the haunted room... there has been formally a park but it is now turned into a farm. However, many of the trees stand and are very beautiful. My mare is neighing at the stable door and I must go to Vallis to see an old lock mended.'

Even at that date it seems that the house needed some repair but was still habitable. The earl had many debts which probably spoilt his plans for any grand restoration and he died in 1762. The great manor became a farm and has been so ever since. In 1844 the local artist William Wheatley sketched the remains of the great hall then in use as a barn with ivy cascading from the roof, bare walls, a rubble strewn floor and a solitary figure sitting beside a grinding wheel in front of a long dead fire.

The Great Hall sketched by WW Wheatley in 1844

Charting the decline of this once magnificent building is no easy task as it appears to have been friendless for centuries, possibly too far from town for the younger generation or too close to their other home at Marston. However, part of it was still occupied in the nineteenth century when in 1864 the Earl of Cork and Orrery entertained a party of geologists from Bath to luncheon. It survived as a carpenters and wheelwrights shop the beautifully made timber and stone roof still resisting all nature's assaults upon it. In 1894 the prolific author and artist Charles R B Barrett[2] sketched the outside and described it as being in a terribly mutilated condition. The erection of a new residence for the tenant farmer in around 1870 near the old house is perhaps an indication that it was not thought to be worth the trouble of restoration. The Earls of Cork and Orrery presided over its decline, selling off the remaining parts in 1905 following the death of the ninth earl.

REMAINS OF VALLIS MANOR-HOUSE, NEAR BATH,

A view from the west in the 1860s showing the hall and private apartments

RUINED MANORHOUSE, VALLIS.

A sketch by CRB Barrett in 1893

The roof was still largely intact in 1928 when Lord Hylton visited with architect Harold Brakspear who wrote,

> The hall retains its open timber roof of the 15th century divided by arched principles into five bays having three perlins on each side supported by curved wind braces. It is covered with stone tiles which are now falling in.[3]

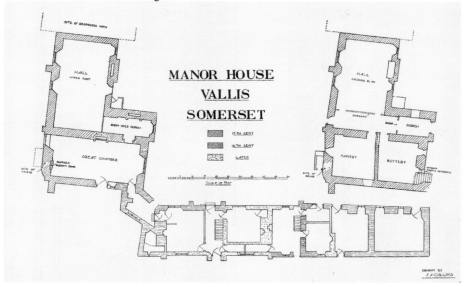

A plan of the remains in 1929

Photographs taken in the mid to late 1950s show the magnificent medieval roof timbers still in place thanks largely to the survival of the stone tiles covering them but these soon went either stolen or sold on and with them went all hope of survival.

Roof of the Great Hall in 1959.
Roger Abbott

There was a concerted campaign by members of the Frome Society during the mid 1970s to try and save what was left of this important building. It was a depressing situation and in 1974 local historian Michael McGarvie was moved to state that, 'The great hall, alas, is beyond salvation as such, but if the remains of the roof were removed and the walls reduced in height it might make a charming walled garden the interior turfed and marked out with such features as the position of the dais and screens passage.

The roof tiles start to fall 1959. Roger Abbott

The fireplace, mediaeval window and entrance archway would remain. The consolidation of the best features is all that we can hope for now.'

McGarvie commenting in the *Somerset Standard* during October of 1974 continued,

It was probably Edmund's grandson William who died in 1485 who built the great hall. Even in the last stages of decay it is a spectacular and noble edifice. It was originally of two storeys and capped with a magnificent open timber roof of which one section survives in situ. Beneath the rafters were those serried lines of curved braces which are such a distinctive feature of mediaeval roofs. The principal rafters are also elegantly braced and the wall posts rest firmly on carved corbels. There are the remains of a cusped window and an arched stone fireplace. William's successes continued to embellish their home during the 16th century, inserting mullioned and transomed windows, a new porch and a southern range of buildings, all on a modest scale.

Stripped of its tiles and near collapse

In October 1978 the remaining land and buildings were divided into lots and auctioned off, the remains of the manor, outbuildings and 4.75 acres of land making £26,000, sold to a Mr Date. Within a year an application for demolition on the grounds of safety was put before Mendip Council who offered to advise on stabilising the walls and discussed the possibility of a grant but found that 'the owner is not prepared to put in more than a nominal sum nor initiate the works'. The application provoked outrage amongst local historians with Dr John Harvey one of the country's leading the mediaevalists describing the threat of demolition as 'monstrous', writing with, 'great concern and distress'.

McGarvie, too, joined in the protests on behalf of the Frome Society, citing not only its architectural importance but outlining its literary connections to Lord Orrery the first biographer of Jonathan Swift, Elizabeth Rowe the eighteenth century poet, Mrs Tuck who wrote a fine poem in its honour in 1823[4] as well as pioneering historians and antiquarians, Rev. William Phelps, Rev. John Skinner and the artist WW Wheatley.

McGarvie continues, 'the gable of the chamber is still a striking feature and has an eight light mullioned and transomed window, (now blocked) of around 1600. Until recent months the great chamber had substantial remains of its mediaeval roof and we regret to say that this has now disappeared; the whole structure is a significant example of a mediaeval manor house and its development and adaption in the sixteenth century and later.' He concluded that the Frome Society considered Vallis Manor House to be of architectural and historical interest, 'facts already recognised by its inclusion in a statutory list as a grade II building. It also considers the building to be of archaeological importance and to have significant literary associations it has a future role to play in the fields of amenity and education the society considers that the application to demolish the remains should be refused'.[5]

The final nail in the coffin seems to be a letter from Andrew Saunders, Chief Inspector of Ancient Monuments for the Department of the Environment to John Harvey in March of 1979 in which he states,

'I have now seen the site and must confess that it really has gone too far and guardianship by Department is out of the question. The best thing I can suggest is encouraging the local authority to take some form of limited stabilisation. We are hoping to meet to the council to discuss the possibilities but I am not optimistic of results. It is extraordinary that this building was not appreciated in the past while something might have been done to save it'.

Mary-Rose Leversedge negotiates the ruins of her ancestors mansion in 1985 [6]

A farewell visit was arranged by the Frome Society as part of an evening walk around Vallis and the demolition went ahead but spared a pleasantly restored range of stone cottages with a few of the manor walls remaining in the grounds now forming part of the gardens.[7]

All that remains. In the grounds of Vallis Manor Cottage

[1] McGarvie *The Book of Frome* p.36
[2] CRB Barrett *Somersetshire: Highways, Byways and Waterways* 1894
[3] SANHS Proceedings Lord Hylton Volume 74 1929
[4] *Frome Yearbook 5* for 1993 Frome Museum
[5] Letter to Mendip Council 11 December 1978 Frome Museum.
[6] Leversedge & Patton: A Family History. Kate Harry. Frome Museum
[7] *Frome Yearbook 12* for 2008 page 36-37 inc photo 1959 p.481 Frome Museum

ELIZABETH TUCK (1789-1861)

Poet, Bookseller and Political Activist

John Millns

An earlier article, confirmed that Elizabeth Tuck was one of six children born in Frome to John Tuck (1751-1818), the bookbinder, printer and bookseller of Whittox Lane and his wife Mary Lane. From an early age, Elizabeth worked in the family business alongside her sister Mary and brothers John and Stephen Tuck.[1] Recent research has revealed that following her father's death, Elizabeth continued to assist the family with the bookselling side of the business while devoting more time to her passion for poetical writing.[2 and 3]

Elizabeth Tuck was the author of *The Juvenile Poetical Moralist* published as a half-bound new edition and reviewed by the *Evangelical Magazine* in 1820 followed by her classic anthology *Vallis Vale and other Poems* in 1823.[4] This later collection of her nineteen poems printed by Crockers of Frome extended over 110 pages and was published in hardback by Longman, Hurst, and Co of Paternoster Row (now Longman Pearson) and sold for five shillings by booksellers in London, Bath and by M and S Tuck in Frome.[4]

VALLIS VALE,

AND

Other Poems.

BY THE AUTHOR OF
" THE JUVENILE POETICAL MORALIST."

Elizabeth Tuck

" O, if such scenes thou lov'st,
Scorn not the minstrel strain."
Sir Walter Scott.

Detail from the title page of Elizabeth's anthology acquired by Rev F J Stainforth, a mid nineteenth century London collector of British and American female authors' work.[5]

A review at that time in the *Imperial Magazine* observed Elizabeth's poems were 'uniformly of a moral and religious nature, calculated to awaken the sensibilities of the heart, and to strengthen the social feelings of our common nature.' Her principal poem *Vallis Vale* presented numerous legendary tales set in the ancient Vallis landscape beside the winding Mells Stream as it flowed through the Vale towards the hamlet of Hapsford about a mile northwest of Frome. Verses tell of historical events from the earliest Druidic days to the visit by St Aldhelm, the Abbot of Malmesbury in the seventh century and later 'snippets well known to the native inhabitants of the neighbourhood' who gathered in the Vale for recreation, courtship and musical parties during the summer months. Several verses referenced a 'Seraphic Rowe,' who lived in Frome and at one time had a house adjoining the Vale with a nearby cave under one of the rock outcrops known locally as 'Mrs Rowe's grotto'.[4]

As readers will recall, 'Mrs Rowe' was the well-known and admired eighteenth century poet and essayist Elizabeth Singer Rowe (1674–1737). Almost a century later, Elizabeth Tuck's poetical works were published anonymously which may explain why she has been comparatively overlooked for so long as one of Frome's celebrated women poets and writers of the nineteenth century. It is believed the name 'Elizabeth Tuck' seen on the volume's inner title page above was written by the Rev Francis J Stainforth as the distinctive writing matched that in his *Catalogue of the Library of Female Authors* covering four centuries of literary history. See his two handwritten entries below credited to Elizabeth Tuck: H4 *Vallis Vale and other poems 1823* and E8 her nineteen pieces in *Selwood Wreath* an extensive volume of selected Frome verse edited by Charles Bayly and published in 1841 by James Burns, London.

The two entries credited to the poetical work of Frome's Elizabeth Tuck in Stainforth's
'Catalogue of the Library of Female Authors.'[5]

After Stainforth's death and the auction of his vast collection, his copy of *Vallis Vale and other Poems,* with his label attached to the end leaf, was acquired by the British Museum and later by The British Library.[5] Bayly's volume *Selwood Vale* contained three hundred and ten poems including nineteen by Elizabeth Tuck along with many by Mrs Rowe, Bishop Ken and numerous other learned people with varying degrees of merit from the neighbourhood. Frome Heritage Museum has a rare first edition – ref L186.

The two final verses below are from Elizabeth Tuck's extended poem *Evening* seen on the last page of her 1823 anthology.[6] As with much of her literary style during this period of her life, her works revealed a strong religious faith combined with a romantic fascination with the natural world, heaven and immortality.

Then is he blest, supremely blest,

    Hope stands on tiptoe, plumed for flight,

And Faith surveys the wondrous rest,

    And Glory, bends from worlds of light,

While in her hand that crown she brings,

    Worn only where her favourites be ;

Beckons, and smiles, and claps her wings,

    And whispers, "Immortality."

This first edition of Elizabeth Tuck's 'Vallis Vale and other Poems' was originally held in the Stainforth Library, (by the museum's stamp) and is now in The British Library [5]

Crockers, Printers, Frome.

Shortly after Elizabeth's publication of *Vallis Vale* and the death of her mother in 1825, the Tuck family cottage on Whittox Lane was sold and by 1827 sisters Elizabeth and Mary owned and occupied a larger well-appointed cottage a few doors away believed to have been the currently named *'The Old Bakehouse'* opposite Zion Chapel.[2] By this time, brothers John and Stephen Tuck traded as bookbinders and printers from their premises nearby.[1 and 2] Mary married the following year to live and work in London's china trade which left Elizabeth trading as E Tuck Bookseller from Whittox Lane. She continued her poetical writing with thirteen new poems published along with several earlier pieces in Bayly's *Selwood Wreath*.

After many years as a member of Frome's Badcox Lane Baptist Chapel, Elizabeth Tuck joined the Zion Congregationalists in 1837 and from around that time she also became a 'fervent member' and activist for the Anti-Corn Law League political movement which sought to abolish the statutes levied taxes on imported wheat. She led a local team of fund-raisers whose combined efforts from canvassing, organizing bazaars and a local arts and crafts exhibition based on the theme free trade raised an impressive £125 towards the League's national campaign. The Corn Laws were finally repealed in 1846 leading to the lowering of prices of wheat and bread for the nation's working population and for the impoverished people in Frome.[8]

In later years, Elizabeth traded books from Catherine Hill while her celebrated poem *The World we have not seen* was adapted as the Congregationalist hymn *There is a region lovelier far that sages tell or poets Sing,* published in 1857 as seen in the Victorian needlework sampler below. During the second half of the nineteenth century her poem was published in hymn books of thirty-two different non-conformist denominations and in numerous other publications.[7] As with all Elizabeth Tuck's literary work, most were still published anonymously.

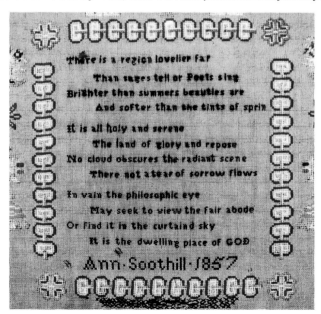

Detail of the needlework sampler by schoolgirl Ann Soothill in 1857 illustrates verses of Elizabeth Tuck's celebrated hymn 1058 under the title 'Heaven' published in *The Congregational Hymn Book*' of 1857 and later in many other non-conformist hymnaries.[7]

A signed first edition of *Vallis Vale and other Poems* is held in the Armstrong Browning Library's growing *'Women Poets Collection'* at Baylor University, Texas. Their collection's emphasisis on nineteenth century British poets of merit included Christina Rossetti of Frome fame. Other first editions of Elizabeth Tuck's anthology are held in the Bodleian Library, Oxford and in numerous American University Libraries including Yale, UC Davis, Emery and Stanford.[5] Frome Heritage Museum also has the first edition – ref L2427.

Unpatronized and unknown by the learned and the great, the author presents her little Volume to a candid public; whose decisions in literary cases are seldom ungenerous, and against which there lies no appeal.

Elizabeth Tuck's striking signature under the poignant last paragraph of her anthology's preface page vi.

Armstrong Browning Library, Baylor University, Texas.

Today, still relatively 'unpatronized and unknown by the learned and the great,' Miss Elizabeth Tuck, author of *Vallis Way* and other poetical works, died in 1861 aged 71 at New-buildings,[9] and was buried in Vallis Road Cemetry. Maybe the time has come for the author to take her rightful place alongside the 'Celebrated Women of Frome.'

(A second rare signed first edition of Elizabeth Tuck's *Vallis Vale and other Poems* was sold in 2020 for £350 by Simon Beattie FSA, Antiquarian Bookseller of Chesham, Buckinghamshire.[8] A facsimile reprint in paperback is available today from Amazon for under £20).

[1] Five Generations of the Tuck Family, *Frome Yearbook,* Vol 24, p72

[2] Heads of Households Surveys of Frome, 1785, 1827 and 1835

[3] *Pigot's Directory for Frome, 1822, 1830, 1842 and 1844*

[4] *Vallis Vale, and other Poems,* 1823, Elizabeth Tuck, published by Longman, Hurst, and Co, London.

[5] *Catalogue of the Library of Female Authors*, p459, Rev F J Stainforth, London https://stainforth.scu.edu/stainforths-library-catalog-transcription

[6] *Evening* from *Vallis Vale, and other Poems*, 1823, p102, Elizabeth Tuck

[7] *The Congregational Hymn Book,* number 1058, adapted from Elizabeth Tuck's poem *The World we have not Seen,* p 73 www.hymnary.org/hymn/CHBS1857/1059

[8] *Firsts at London's Rare Book Fair,* 2019, p47, Simon Beattie FSA http://simonbeattie.co.uk/wp-content/uploads/2010/09/At-Firsts-London June-2019.pdf

[9] *Frome Times,* 16 October 1861, Microfilm, Frome Library

Many thanks to Frome Museum, Frome Historical Research Group and Frome Library.

DR FRANCIS BUSH OF FROME 1776-1843

John Webb Singer

In Yearbook 22 David Smart introduced us to the Bush family and outlined their history but many years before, in 1893 Frome industrialist John Webb Singer wrote an article in his series of 'Frome Worthies' for the Somerset Standard: -

There have been three surgeons of this name, the family having been in Frome in this profession from the very beginning of the century, the last having been Mr Edmund Bush who died not many years since but was no relation of Mr F Bush, he having, with Dr White as partner, succeeded to the practice on the death of Francis John Bush in the year 1843, this Mr John being the son of the surgeon of whom a few words may be said as one of the Worthies of Frome.

His monument in the old church tells us that he commenced his work before the end of the last century in 1797 continuing it for 46 years, his fame having been great as the friend and physician of the poor as well as the rich. If you ask any poor persons about 70 years of age whether they knew, 'Old Dr Bush,' if a man he will very likely say, 'Oh! yes he cut off my brothers leg.' If the question is put to a woman she is almost sure to tell you, 'Yes! He helped my sister, (or some other relation) out of her troubles'. It is very rarely that a surgeon has ever been so popular and widely known as was Dr Francis Bush for he was clever, ready and fearless in his profession and so genial in his manner that very many sought his counsel and advice, especially the poor as he lived when parish doctors had a very different position to those of the present time, the Board of Guardians and having been first appointed only six years before Mr Bush's death and he, in contending with these gentlemen, came to a sad end.

Knoll House in Gentle Street

Mr Bush senior resided, and long practised his profession, in Gentle Street in the house where Mr Pulham now has a school, his only son, Francis John, living in Knoll House opposite which was built for them on the marriage of his son. Mr Bush was said to be rather fond of what is called, 'bricks and mortar', once buying a house at Fromefield, which has since been called Spring Hill. This house he remodelled and almost rebuilt then selling it to Miss Susan Sheppard who much annoyed the doctor by pulling it entirely down before anyone had lived in it and on the same spot she built the present house. One of his smart sayings as to this place has been preserved, for, seeing a mason doing his work carelessly and then using a good deal of bad mortar in which too much dirt had been put with which to cover it up, he said, 'Ah! I see your business is something like mine, where the dirt often hides a good deal of bad work,' alluding to the patients that got buried from a doctors mistake. In Mr Bush's time, medical education was not so easy to attain as at present and there being a butcher's killing place near in Gentle Street he would often take his pupils there and explain to them the several organs of the animals when cut up.

Mr Bush married a lady of good family the daughter of Captain Edgell and the sister of Mr Edgell who once lived at East Hill House. (Lucrecia Dorothy Edgell 1764-1842). She was the doctors senior by about 12 years and was the widow of a military gentleman named Jones. In her day she was famous as the best dressed lady in Frome; in fact, leading the fashions in this town and was always watched and admired when the new fashions came out she being the guide for many. Although she lived to be much over 70 years of age, to the end of her days she so dressed herself up that if you only saw her from behind you would imagine seeing a young lady not over 25 years old, the front view being very much less deceptive and gaining for herself the title of the, 'Butterfly of Frome'

The old lady boasted to the end of her life that she had royal blood in her veins. Mrs Jones had, by her first husband, one daughter who died in her 25th year after her mother became Mrs Bush. She had only one son by her second marriage. Mrs Bush was of a totally opposite temperament to her husband, as he would do anything for the poor, often taking up in his conveyance a person carrying a heavy basket to market, whereas Mrs Bush dreaded any poor person coming near her and children, knowing this, would run against her for the reproof it brought down on them. It is doubtful whether there was much sympathy between the doctor and his wife as he was heard to say that if he ever married again he should like his wife to first come on trial to learn her opinion. Yet within a year of her death he unsuccessfully sought the affections of a rich spinster in Catherine Hill. As a surgeon Mr Bush was bold and daring in his surgical work there being, in his day few of the class now called specialists and thus people did not go up to London for operations as they now do, the most serious cases being treated in the country, to the great advantage of provincial doctors who had the fame which Mr Bush acquired, all sorts of operations being reported of him.

Both Mr Bush and his son were celebrated for the treatment of cancer, and many persons with this disease came to Frome for their assistance in this calamity remaining at lodgings so as to be near and under their care. Although often kind in manner, Mr Bush was still far more pronounced and outspoken than the present style of the medical profession. Thus, to one patient to whom he was called who had symptoms of dropsy he said,

Dr Francis Bush

"You must take care, for you may be gone in a moment like the snuff of a candle or you may last 20 years," which time the patient did really live.

To another patient with an uncommon malady he said,

"I never had but five such cases, two of them I killed and three I saved"

A respectable lad requiring a tooth to be extracted did not behave quite to the doctors liking, and while taking out the tooth he gave him a box on the ear to behave better. Once a man went to the surgery pretending to have something the matter with his shoulder having his arm bound up in a sling. The doctor got his coat off and finding there was nothing to complain of kicked him down the steps in front of the surgery. He was sent for to a farmhouse in the country to see a patient who was thought to require bleeding, this being the age of phlebotomy, but he had forgotten to bring his lancet; nothing daunted he borrowed the implement that farmers used for bleeding the calves and horses and soon performed the operation.

Of young Mr Bush, it is said a man went to him complaining that he had lost the sense of smell entirely; telling him where he lived, which was a place of bad reputation as to the odours there the doctor said to him, "Go home! go home! my good man and be thankful" many such anecdotes can be related of this firm; very strong words often being mixed up with them.

The father and son were long in partnership together and so great was their practice that few country doctors kept such a stable of horses as did Dr Bush and his son; they attended patients far and wide and these doctors were of the few in the profession that swallowed up more than the usual share of the practice around them. The popularity of Mr Bush having the result that not a few of his clients wished to have a copy of his portrait, a painting of him having been taken by Townsend. This was reproduced by John Hunt in a steel engraving after the style of the annuals of his time and the same is now to be found in many houses in Frome showing him to have a fine open-faced countenance; the portraits sold at five shillings each.

The doctor first commenced his practice and lived in the old house next to the Packhorse Inn, and there are now old men living in Frome who, as boys, went to that place with their parents for the then annual visits by many for the operation of bleeding, which it was considered healthful to have done each spring. It is now only 60 years ago when the value of this operation began to be questioned, and many doctors took opposite sides of the dispute, Dr Bush being one of those who gave up the practice, although at one time it was part of the remedy for many diseases. The doctor had a patient at Leighton named Budgett who was not quite satisfied with his treatment giving him up for a Dr Bushman of a neighbouring town who bled his patients very copiously. Budgett, soon after, dying, which led to a most angry correspondence between these rival doctors being published, the tone of which was very bitter. Among other things Dr Bush had the following lines of his own composition printed by Mr Penny and circulated as if the conversation of Dame Nature with Dr Bushman,

DAME NATURE AND THE PHYSICIAN

Old Lady

 Nine teacups of blood, and all taken at once;
And leeching besides, what a consummate DUNCE!
The blood is his life, while it flows in the veins,
And 'tis this simple fact so clearly explains
Why, when drained from the man and out in the cup,
The man gave a sob, and the game was soon up;
Believe me, dear doctor, with grief and surprise,
I witnessed your practice, and death take his prize.

Doctor

Madam, dare you then assume this impudent strain,
Pray mind your own business-this job is mine
The man may revive - and I'll bleed him again .

Old Lady

The case is a bad one – with sorrow 'tis said
His life's in the teacups - his spirit is fled!
Tho' blessed with your skill, he's just pass'd the bourne
Which ends all his travels – he'll never return.
Since again we may meet, I'll give you a hint
(I'm sure 'tis a good one and worthy of print),
With spectacles on, still a man maybe blind;
So let me take the lead, and you shove behind.

Doctor

You impertinent Jade, you always go wrong;
Read my Certificates! - and then hold your tongue.
My practice is such - It is sure to succeed,
I bleed them - I bleed them as long as they'll bleed

Mr William Davis who was then clerk to the magistrates of Frome, and a literary person, took up the question and, among other pieces wrote,

When professors of science begin to dispute,

They neither promote or advance it;
But, if bleeding is the subject they intend to confute,
Let them publish their thoughts in the *Lancet.*

It was, especially as the poor man's doctor that many admired and looked up to Dr Bush, and it was on their behalf, and for them, that he finished his work and died. At this date Guardians had not long been in existence and whether they were harsh or not cannot now be told, but they must have had a busy time of it, as the great workhouse for the Union had just been built in Frome, instead of the old house for the poor which formally stood on the spot where Mr C Bayly now lives, Clumber House.

At this time, a great outcry came as to the bread the new Guardians provided for the poor, and Mr Bush procured one of these loaves taking it from where he lived to the room opposite, where the Guardians then met, intending to enter a warm protest against it before the whole body. The excitement of this proceeding, whilst cutting up the loaf, brought on a fit of apoplexy, and the poor doctor fell down dead in the room before the whole Board of Guardians.

This naturally caused a great excitement the cause of it stirring up the feelings of many so that his funeral was a demonstration of respect the like of which had not been seen for nearly 50 years, and there has been nothing like it since until the late vicar's funeral took place, as hundreds followed the corpse to the grave and thousands watched the procession. The vault in which he is buried is just within the central west doors of the parish church and he and his son, who died and followed him to the grave only seven weeks afterwards, were nearly the last persons buried in the church.

The epitaphs on the Bush monument may interest some as it is not easy to read them where they are placed:-

> Sacred to the memory of Francis Bush who died September 19th 1843 aged 67. For 46 years a surgeon in this town. In his profession he was skilful, kind and unwearied. The esteem in which he was held, and the regret for his sudden death, were testified on the day of his internment when more than 400 persons followed his remains to the grave.
> Also Dorothy Lucrecia, daughter of Captain Edgell and wife of the above who died June 30 1842 aged 78.

WALTER GARRETT 1873-1900

A Short, Eventful Life

ALM

Walter Garrett was born in Frome to parents Charles and Louise (née Thorne) Garrett. His father was a brush manufacturer and in 1900 they were living at Box Villa, Keyford. There were seven children. After completing his education Walter Garrett was employed by J W Singer as a draughtsman's apprentice. In September 1889 the family's house and shop at 7 Keyford was destroyed by fire. Walter was 16 and was awakened in the early hours by his father and told the house was on fire and to awaken the servant girl. He went up to her room and caught hold of her hand and pulled her from bed. They went onto the landing but she decided to get dressed before escaping and returned to her bedroom. Walter, dressed only in his shirt, escaped from the house by an upstairs window onto a lower roof and then went to the police station and raised the alarm. The servant, Annie Moore, aged 21, died, and was found fully clothed and wearing her shoes. She was badly burnt about her upper body. At the inquest a fireman witness recalled that there had been two previous fires at the premises and by repute 'four or five.' The coroner said that Annie had 'sacrificed her life to her feelings of modesty.'

In May 1892 a boy named French (probably Albert French born 1885 of Blue Boar Yard) slipped from the bank of the river Frome into deep water. The mother of one of his friends, Mrs Gunston also of the Blue Boar Yard, was called and went into the river to rescue him but got into difficulty and both were submerged. The incident was seen by Walter Garrett from Singer's offices. He rushed down to the river bank and into the river and with the help of others pulled the two to safety. A columnist in the local paper called for donations to a fund to mark the bravery of Mrs Gunston but after two weeks only 2/- had been received; the writer expressed his disappointment as he was suggesting contributions of just 6d. Subsequently a woman donated 2/6d - no mention was found of further contributions.

In November 1897 Walter Garrett was in his office at Singers when, he 'noticed a girl struggling in the river which at that point was about 10ft deep. He immediately ran down and without divesting himself of any clothes jumped in and swam to the girl who was in the middle of the stream and after much difficulty succeeded in reaching the bank.' (*Somerset & Wilts Journal*)

At a ceremony at Easter 1898 of the local Buffalo Lodge at the Bull Hotel, Mr H T Rawlings presented Walter Garrett with a vellum certificate in an oak frame from the Royal Humane Society. The citation said that his 'courage and humanity saved the life of Lizzie Freeman.' Garrett was a good all-round athlete and at one time captained the Frome Rugby 2nd XV.

When the 2nd Boer War started in 1899 he volunteered and joined the Wilts Imperial Yeomanry leaving for South Africa in January 1900. Garrett was killed at Leeuw River Mills on 4 September 1900.Trooper W E Dalby, also of the 'Wilts', in a letter to his brother Dr Dalby of Frome witnessed Garrett's death: 'On Monday 3rd September about 1,000 men were camped about three miles from Leeuw River including the Cameron Highlanders. The following morning the Chief of Police of Thabu Nchu asked for eight men to accompany him and his men to capture 20 Boers near Leeuw River. Le Gros and Garrett were amongst the eight. I was on a hill and had a pretty good view of what happened. The Boers were surprised and so were our men as they found them where they did not expect.' Here Dalby's version differs from Mrs Bateman's account below; he maintains that the Boers fired first. '...the Boers were firing at our men within a 20 yard range and Garrett, who had fallen off his horse, was just getting up when a soft nosed Mauser bullet struck him in the throat, killing him at once.....Corey was wounded and died the same night... it was awfully sad about Garrett as he came from Frome and as I had known him for four years we had palled a lot together out here, and he was always such a jolly fellow. When I found it was him they had killed, I can tell you it knocked me a bit, and we wondered if the game was worth the candle.'

Mrs Bateman, wife of a local miller who lived close to where the incident took place, wrote a letter to Garrett's parents:

> It is with a sad heart I address you to tell you what you doubtless know ere this, your dear one is no more. Poor dear Garrett, we all I may say, loved him... He was here some time...the Company moved to Thaba Nchu... A Boer patrol came about 9.30 on the eve of the 3rd... I got up at 6.30 next morning, and they asked for breakfast. It was sent out to them. The Captain sent for me. I went out, and he asked me what he owed me. I said 'Oh nothing,' and asked where they were going. He said 'To retake Thaba Nchu.'... After thanking me for my kindness I turned to go in, when 'Bang Bang' went a bullet. I said 'What's that'? and he said the British. The Boers were then saddling up. I said 'No, don't fire; there are no British here', when 'Bang, Bang went the bullets and helter-skelter the Boer horses.' Even then I failed to see any British, but, poor fellows, they were there... Miss Findlay rushed out under fire to Corey, who fell shot through both lungs. He lived, poor fellow 13 hours... I hurriedly prepared all beds.... Then they said Le Gros had fallen. We sent another couch, and fetched in an Australian. It was not Le Gros... Then the next couch brought poor Mr Garrett, at the same time Dr Bruce came galloping up. We had Corey in bed, and had cut off the trousers of the Australian, who was wounded in the thigh.
>
> I went along to poor Garrett. I took his hands and said 'Mr Garrett poor Mr Garrett,' hoping he was not dead. Our coachman said 'It's no use Missus, he is quite dead.' I rushed out, and saw Dr Bruce, saying, 'First come here Doctor, those are being attended to perhaps this poor fellow is not quite dead.' He touched him and turned him, saw a small hole under the right ear and a big ragged one under the left... Dr Bruce said 'Come away Mrs Bateman it's no sight for you, you can do nothing.' but I lingered by his side still hoping for some faint sign of life but in vain. Sir Thomas Fowler[1] wanted him buried at once, but I objected and begged leave to have him properly attended to and buried by the Wesleyan Minister of Ladybrand. All that could be done, was done poor fellow. We had many pleasant hours with him...All who knew him loved him even the natives. Oh! I cannot tell you how I felt when I stood beside his graveside...... I will care for his grave and send you a photograph of it soon. Oh, my heart is so sore and sad; poor fellow, I liked him so well.... I shall be coming home soon and can tell you more.

The last letter from Garrett addressed to Mr A Edwards was written on 26 August and received one week after his death:

> Although I have not written to you lately, no doubt you have heard from Mr Lawes how I've been having a good time lately. Eight of us were selected to take 65 prisoners to Wepener. They had to walk the whole way and some of the poor fellows were awfully sore footed and could hardly hobble along so we let them ride our horses occasionally. The ages ranged from 74 to 14. Every night we sang songs to them which they enjoyed. On entering Wepener we met the Royal Scots who were leaving for Bloemfontein. They had their band playing and it sounded a treat. One of our fellows rode up to the Colonel and asked if we should halt and let his regiment pass or should we go on. He had his men lined up either side of the road and told us to take the prisoners through. The remarks from the Tommies were not altogether choice ones... It was not nice for the prisoners to listen to. When we arrived at Wepener and handed the prisoners over the Commissioner told us he would find a guard over them for the night so that we could have a good sleep. Off we went to the Hotel, but it was closed owing to one of the Scots being found drunk the night before. So I went to the Commissioner and asked if we might have a drink and he gave us permission to have what we wanted. The next day we were informed that we had to

take the prisoners to Smithfield, a two-day march. After giving over the prisoners we wanted something to eat, but only had a few shillings, so I trotted off to the manager of the hotel and sold him a buc (sic) for 12/6 I had killed. Even then we hadn't enough for a decent spread. We explained the situation to the Commissioner who gave us £3 and told us to have a drink and a box of cigarettes at his expense. So, we had a large Bass each. I wonder what he thought when he came to settle up.

To our surprise we were told to take the prisoners to Rouxville, a two day march. The Commissioner being a bit of a sportsman treated us well and made us all drunk himself included…We had a high time at Zastion, we stayed two days. I went to a house the first night and the gent showed me De Wet's [2] photo. I asked him to give it to me but he would not, so I got him busily engaged in conversation and put it in my pocket forgetting to give it back again. I came away and would not stop for supper. I showed it to Sir Thomas Fowler and he wanted it, but no I would not part so have sent it home to Arthur[3]. I hope it will reach him safely and now I am back at camp and shall be glad when it is all over.

Walter Garrett received the Queen's South African Medal with clasps: Cape Colony and Orange Free State, posthumously. His colleagues at Singers designed and made a bronze memorial plaque in his honour which was placed in Sheppard's Barton church on a white marble slab. The bronze plaque is now in Frome Museum.

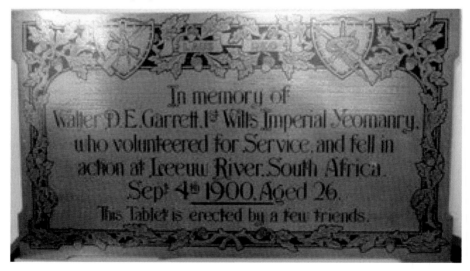

The *Somerset Standard* of 26 December 1900 described the plaque as follows:

'The ornamentation and inscription are engraved. On the border above the inscription the implements of peace and war are beautifully depicted. The left-hand shield displays the materials of the deceased man's craft, his compass, pencil, T square and scroll. The shield on the opposite side depicts the weapons etc of a cavalryman.'

[1]Captain Sir Thomas Fowler, Bart. Born 1868. Killed in action and also the 20 April 1902 at Oliver's Farm Moolman Spruit, Flicksburg.

[2] De Wet -1854-1922 Boer General, born Smithfield District, Orange Free State.

[3] Arthur H Garrett, brother aged 37, Hairdresser & Tobacconist at Trowbridge.

VE DAY, 8 MAY 1945

This charming memoir comes from Mark Pattinson whose mother Audrey Millward was evacuated to Frome from Southsea with her sister Ruth. Being so close to the large naval base at Portsmouth the area was heavily bombed and her policeman father was bombed out at least twice. Audrey stayed at Rodden Farm with her aunt and uncle, members of the well-known Crees farming family. After the war she returned to the Southsea area but she had so enjoyed the farming life as an evacuee that she went on to agricultural college and eight years later, in 1953, returned with her husband Dennis Pattinson to Rodden Farm for the rest of her life.

'We had a holiday from school, went into Frome in the afternoon on bikes to see flags and listen to a service in St John's outside. Frome decorated with flags. At 7.00 we went to a thanksgiving service in church. About 11.30 we lit a huge bonfire top of Homeground (it was

a cart-load of straw). The Hawkins came along, Jimmy Crees and Graham Gillard. There were flashes, fireworks, search lights, bonfires and flares during the night.

Uncle went into Frome Tuesday night, he said they were very drunk and standing on top of cars, etc. and the Americans threw money and chewing gum in the air for everyone to pick up. They took hold of Sam Minty because he was in police uniform and poured beer into his mouth and they brought out glasses of beer and broke the glasses against the cars and walls.

On Wednesday we went to market but there were no shops open. At 11 o'clock went to a service at St Johns in Frome. We went into Frome at about 10, watched the crowd in the Market Place singing and dancing, nobody was drunk as the pubs had sold out the night before.

Audrey Millward aged 14.

We saw the flood lighting. We went to bed both nights about one o'clock. We put a flag on the barn and on the cart house, three in the garden and three in the little garden by the yard.'

At Work on the Farm

THE FOLKLORE OF FROME

Lisa Kenright

Introduction

Somerset is known for having a rich tradition of folk tales and legends. However, closer study of the main books about Somerset folklore and folk tales shows that while there are stories about screaming skulls to the south of us here in Frome, dragons and King Arthur to the west and the Fair Folk in more or less every direction, there is a dearth of tales from Frome itself. Westwood and Simpson's *Lore of the Land* (2005) has a map for each county with jaunty symbols for the different classes of tale. There are a few witches' hats and a scattering of other types in the east of Somerset, but the vast majority of dragons, buried treasure and other legends are clustered south and west of a line between Bridgwater and Cadbury Castle. I have been researching why that might be and also looking for any information that might have been missed in the main collections.

This article is intended to be the first part of a report on a survey of folklore connected to Frome. Here I introduce the main sources for folklore in the county of Somerset and collect together those items that they found specifically in, or about, this town. The second part will be on the stories and lore I have found from other sources. I hope to use this information as a baseline for further research in the future.

Firstly, we need to define what is meant by the word 'folklore'. The OED says it is: 'The traditional beliefs, legends, and customs, current among the common people; the study of these.' The word was first coined (as 'folk-lore') in 1846 by WJ Thoms in place of the older term 'popular antiquities' with the explicit intention to reference 'manners, customs, observances, superstitions, ballads, proverbs…of olden time' (*The Athenaeum* 1846 quoted in Simpson and Roud 2000, p130). Originally the element 'folk' did not mean everyone in a society, or even all the non-elites, but specifically the rural, illiterate poor. Material culture such as crafts were also excluded with the emphasis on oral tradition. From the middle of the twentieth century the definition changed and expanded so that folklorists now study informal information circulated by members of any group by whatever media. This last is particularly important as folklore researchers are now more aware of the interplay between written and oral sources as, while folk tales are once again being re-told orally, they are only there waiting to be found because someone wrote them down. The internet is now also an important arena for creating and passing on such knowledge.

Once, perhaps seen as just twee tales of the Fair Folk and quaint customs about cider orchards, the definition has now expanded to include many different aspects of life including: material culture, such as folk magic objects and crafts; actions such as traditions, rituals and calendar customs; word-based culture such as sayings, games and stories. For this article I will be focussing on the latter two categories. Folk music and songs can also be included however this is a huge area that needs to be studied separately.

So now we move on to the Somerset folklore collections that I included in the survey. In some counties the early collecting of folklore in the late nineteenth century involved genteel scholars, mostly men but some women, going out into the countryside deliberately to record ancient lore. However more often, authors collected items from their own everyday interactions and previous texts as well as snippets sent either directly by acquaintances or via publications such as *Notes & Queries*. Charles Henry Poole's *The Customs, Superstitions, and Legends of the County of Somerset* would fit into this category. Later collectors made more efforts to record information about the informant and in the latter part of the twentieth century it became easier to take recording equipment out into the field. Surprisingly, Ruth Tongue was the first person who could be called a folklorist who attempted to collect items from Somerset, working in the first half of the twentieth century but published mostly in the 1960s. However, she recorded items she came across in her early life from memory and did not collect in a systematic way. Kingsley Palmer did further work in the late 1960s, the only collector I came across who used academic-style, deliberate collecting. However, despite both of these authors publishing books with 'Somerset' in the title, this work was concentrated on parts of the county only, the west in the case of Tongue and the south for Palmer.

As well as surveying the works of Tongue and Palmer for reference to our town, I have also checked any other collections of folklore I could find that might be expected to cover the Frome area, so books covering 'Somerset' were included but those covering 'Exmoor' were ignored. Similarly, while I have included collections of 'folklore', 'legends' or 'folk tales', I have excluded collections of hauntings and ghost stories, curiosities, murders and true crime. Though some ghost tales can be called folklore, most, so-called 'real' hauntings, are not. True-life crime, particularly murder, is one area where the town does feature a great deal. However, while local tales about crimes may become folklore, passed from person to person, growing as they go, the factual description of historically provable events cannot, so they too have been set aside.

National Collections of Folklore

When looking for local folklore, many begin with the classic national collections of local legends. Although not specific to Somerset, they are arranged by county so are easy to check for material on a specific community.

Folklore Myths and Legends of Britain by The Readers Digest has become a legend in its own right among folklore enthusiasts and if you are interested in the subject it is well worth the few pounds it will cost you in a charity shop. Each county section begins with a map to show the location of the items of folklore with symbols to show whether you are looking for a ghost, a witch, buried treasure or so on. It is therefore easy to see that the closest items to us in the Somerset chapter are from Shepton Mallet (p162 for the full entry), with a version of the Cannard's Grave story and the tale of Nancy Camel. Neither mention Frome, but some versions of the former tale include the people of this town. See below for more on this story.

Cley Hill with its Bronze Age barrow in the centre.

As Wiltshire is so close it is always worth looking at that chapter as well and there is a version of the story about how Cley Hill was created by the Devil (p174). This tale is in several guide books, though a longer more ornate version. Sadly, no sources are given for any of the material in this publication so it is difficult to trace this tale back from here. This tale fits into a wider genre of supernatural beings creating various landscape features across Britain, such as the similar story from Sussex about Devil's Dyke. They are regarded as relatively recent, mostly being dated from the eighteenth century or later. There are also possibly earlier tales with giants in the same role. See the tales of the Giants' Vincent and Gorm creating the Avon Gorge for example. This tale about Cley Hill being one of the few stories that I have been told here in town so I hope to research it further.

The Lore of the Land (Westwood and Simpson 2005) is a rather more academically rigorous collection by two renowned folklorists. It is however arranged in a similar way with its maps and symbols. Shepton Mallet is missed out here but Mells and Nunney are included. The former is represented by the much-repeated, but demonstrably false, tale about the manor's alleged connection with the rhyme 'Little Jack Horner' (p 648) and the latter with the tale of Nunney Hitchhiker (p 649). This story is fascinating in its own right. It follows the pattern of the widely found 'Ghostly (or Vanishing) Hitchhiker' which is often referred to as an Urban Legend but is actually much older than that label suggests, with the earliest versions involving the ghostly figure being given a lift in a horse and cart or carriage. Also mentioned is the Monmouth-related story of how Gibbet Hill got its name. Both of these stories deserve more research and I hope to return to them again. A similar version of the Cley Hill story is repeated in the Wiltshire chapter.

Ruth Tongue

One of the most well-known folklorists that worked in Somerset, Ruth Tongue was born in 1898, the daughter of a minister who settled in Taunton early in her life. Her family moved away when she was still very young and she only returned to the county in her 50s, settling in the Quantocks. Most of the material she collected herself was from the area around Taunton and the northwest Somerset coast. She coined the phrase 'Chime Child' to mean a child born within the hours of midnight and cockcrow on Saturday, an accident of birth that was claimed to give her powers over the supernatural. She made a living as a folklorist later in life, writing several books and articles for the Folklore Society as well as giving talks in person and on the radio but is regarded as 'problematic'. Her claim to be one of the charmed herself hardly made her an impartial observer and this is compounded by the fact she did not in fact spend all of her childhood in Somerset when she claimed to have collected most of her material, leaving around the time she was aged 11. Any notes she did take down were lost in fires and moves so the earlier dates given for her recollections below should be treated with appropriate caution. She often gives no attribution at all and seems to have lifted a great deal from previous writers including Poole. She also found an unusual number of unique stories with no other known versions in the English repertoire and there is a suspicion that she made quite a few of them up from fragments or indeed whole cloth. This would indeed be a terrible fault in a folklore researcher but perfectly normal for what she really was, a storyteller holding on to a world that was nearly gone.

Further discussion on how her tales were collected is not really relevant here, as only one is about this area and that is attested by other writers (the Cannard's Grave tale below). She did however include a few snippets of lore said to be from Frome in her book *Somerset Folklore*

(1965) which was part of the Folklore (then Folk-Lore) Society County Folklore Series. According to Simpson and Roud (2000, p 363) this is considered to be her most reliable book. She does seem to have actually visited Frome herself on at least two occasions: in 1945 when she toured the county on a riding holiday, and in the 1950s when she came to the WI. Several of the snippets are dated 1909 and it is unclear if that is from a school-friend from this area, or if she came here then too, though she would have been around 11 years of age at the time. The rest of the material appears to be collected from Frome natives met elsewhere on her travels.

She tells us about the Orchardleigh Stone (Tongue 1965, p11) whose base no one could find no matter how deep they dug. Tongue used the *Somerset Year Book 1933* as a source, with the additional detail about the stone falling on a labourer being passed on to her by a school-friend in 1909. Presumably this is some local memory about an early excavation on the site, the crushing is likely legendary rather than real. Rather more reliable information about this monument and its excavation can be found in Davis 2020 (pp 56-67). There is another stone-related story on Tongue page 15, about a giant creating a landmark by throwing a rock at Cranmore Church. Although not about this town, it was collected here in 1945.

RELICS of DRUIDISM   ORCHARDLEIGH.

Tongue was very fond of stories about the magic of church bells and includes a famous piece of doggerel said to be on a bell at Frome, made by our very own Cockey.

> God made Cockey,
> And Cockey made me
> In the Year of our Lord
> Seventeen forty three.

(Tongue 1965 p 20, source simply given as '*Eighteenth-century bell*').

There is no such rhyme on any of Frome's bells and none are of the right date. The closest is the bell made by John Lott which has the inscription *I AM HEE FOR JOHN LOTT MADE MEE ANNO DOMINI 1624 (Massey 1985)*. If such a bell exists it is presumably outside of the Frome Deanery as it is not to be found in Massey's book. It has also been claimed for Warminster but I could not find a definite source for that either. Whether or not such a bell really exists, it is still relevant that this bell inscription was thought about and passed on. As folklore, it is almost more interesting if it is entirely a fiction, than if it is merely a misplaced piece of genuine history.

There is an intriguing reference to the Lake Lady of Orchardleigh (p 120), grouped with two other 'White Ladies' from the county that she regards as fairies rather than ghosts. I have been unable to find other references about this tradition, apart from citations of this mention by Tongue. Further research on this piece of folklore would be worthwhile.

There are two references to witchcraft in this area: on page 66 she refers to Julian Cox's trial at Taunton but does not mention that she was from this area. Then on page 226 there is a list of Somerset Witch Trials including the accused witches of Beckington, which she places in Frome. The entry seems somewhat mangled, not least by placing it in the eighteenth century, rather than 1689. She used John Cuming Walters' account from *Bygone Somerset* (1897 p115, the mistake in the century seems to be his). There is a great deal of evidence for belief in witchcraft in this area. The account of Julian Cox's trial gives us an example of the folk tale known as 'The Witch that Was Hurt' (there is a west-Somerset version of this folk tale given on p 71 of Tongue's book) being used as factual evidence. There is also of course our link with Glanvill who was Vicar at St John's. In a separate article in *Folklore* she retells an account by an unnamed woman from a village 'in the Frome area'. She told of another woman in her village who claimed to be able to turn people into 'a tom tit' and who was said to have a mommick (mommet or poppet) to stick thorns into. This is undated but from the 1950s or early 1960s (1963, Vol. 74 No 1 p 323).

Most of the rest of the items collected in this area are sayings and lore. A maidservant at Mells in 1925 advised to sleep under a beech tree if you are lost in a wood at night as then nothing can harm you. If you were going to Frome market in 1909 and saw a magpie, apparently if it was on your right hand you knew your business that day would be lucky, but if it was on the left you would turn around and give up as nothing you did would prosper that day (Frome 1909, p 46). Soak an ivy leaf in vinegar and bind it over a corn on your foot for three days and the corn will come away (p 38, collected in Frome 1957). This advice cropped up on the *Fabulous Folklore* podcast late last year though Frome was not credited and I suspect it is a widespread belief. As always with folk medicine, do not actually try it without expert advice!

There are four undated snippets of wisdom: never let a baby wear green (p 135); get your boots mended on a Tuesday and they'll last twice as long (p 139); If Candlemas Day (2nd February) be fine and clear, Winter will have another year (p 154) and 'people who are born in May are either saintly or turrible wicked bad' (p 165). Again, there is no evidence that these are unique to Frome. There are also two sayings on p 214:

> Rode Revel, Beckington Rout
> The Devil's in Frome and cannot get out

> There was an old cobbler lived in Frome
> And all he wanted was elbow room.

These are about Frome of course, rather than necessarily originating here.

Now we come to the one full narrative shared by Tongue (p 103) that involves Frome, albeit in a walk-on part. The story of Cannards Grave is found in many places including Poole (1877, pp109-10) who refers to Rev. H. Allen, rector of Shepton Mallet in 1692, who mentioned it in his account of the parish bounds. This last is quoted more fully in Farbrother (1872) on page 33. However, this, the earliest mention of the story I could find, only refers to '…a place called Cannard's Grave, because one Cannard, who destroyed himself, as reported, was buried there at the corner of the close there next to the open field…'. The Reverend returns to the subject on p147 and here we find an account so similar to Poole's it would appear that the latter had lifted it almost wholesale from the former. The story at this point was rather simpler than that given in Tongue with the hapless landlord Giles Cannard killing himself fearing he was to be hanged for his sin of forgery. Tongue's version more or less follows this tale but adds detail, including about the people of Frome marching to Shepton in order to hang him themselves. A full account of the different versions of this tale would take a paper by themselves but I have not yet been able to find the involvement of the people of Frome in any other version. This is another interesting story in its own right, being one of the few local legends that seem to have re-entered the oral tradition. I have heard at least four different versions told by professional storytellers acquiring the involvement of highwaymen, Cannard's wife and numerous victims of gruesome murder along the way.

Kingsley Palmer

Kingsley Palmer is now best known for anthropological work in Australia but he began his academic career in Somerset having moved to the Ilminster area as a teen. In the late 1960s he conducted a survey of oral traditions in South Somerset and Dorset. This led to two books of interest here: *Oral Folk-Tales of Wessex* in 1973 and *The Folklore of Somerset* in 1976. The former has a much wider area of interest, extending to Gloucestershire and Cornwall as well as the traditional 'Wessex' counties of Dorset, Somerset and Wiltshire. In the Introduction to *Folklore of Somerset* he admits he has focused on southern Somerset, adding to the work of Ruth Tongue with her focus on the western area. He deliberately did not give even anonymous information about his informants and only occasionally identified where specific items were collected. All of this means, unsurprisingly, that there are only four mentions of the Frome area in the book on Somerset and none in the book on Wessex.

Two of the mentions of the town occur in the section on witches and curses and are both sourced from an article by C. Somerville Watson 'Witchcraft in Somerset' in *Somerset Year Book 1922*. Firstly, in reference to the belief that quicksilver or mercury could counteract spells and curses, Palmer summarizes the account of a man buying mercury from a chemist 'near Frome' (p 62). He wanted to put it in a small case and tie it round his neck because he was bewitched and couldn't sleep. Palmer suggests there was a practical joke going on here, though it is not clear whether it was the bewitched customer, the chemist or a third party he thought was responsible for the 'joke'. It is worth taking a moment to examine the original which has additional detail missing in Palmer. Somerville Watson presents this item as an anecdote that happened during his boyhood with his eldest brother a witness. It is written in dialect as is the style with this publication and is said to have taken place in a chemist's shop in, not near, Frome in the nineteenth century, presumably the latter part.

The second mention of Frome in Palmer is on the next page (p 63) and is a reference to the swimming of a witch at Woodlands in 1730. There is a fuller discussion of the historical context of this incident in Pickering pp 228-9 which also quotes the near-contemporary account from the *Gentleman's Magazine* of 1731 in full. It should be remembered that far from being a 'fairy tale', such historic accounts of witchcraft belief are about the harm done to real people. In this case, the victim of the mob's attack died and three of the perpetrators were charged with manslaughter. The location of Woodlands is not in the older source and may have been introduced by Somerville Watson. This was nearly 50 years after the last legal execution for witchcraft in England. There is also mention of recourse to 'a cunning man', someone who countered spells, and to the hanging of a witch bottle to counter the bewitchment.

gencku nonnct le uofilt a aliranore.

Mumming crops up as an important area of research in many folklore studies. Palmer lists the town along with Stone [sic] Easton, Kilmersdon and Castle Cary as areas where mumming was well established at the beginning of the twentieth century (p 140). We know from a court case that there were mummers here in the seventeenth century and performed at Christmas, but that does not mean the tradition continued uninterrupted. This is another area that would probably reward future study. Palmer also mentions the story of Cannard's Grave on page 89 but he has taken this from Poole's version which does not include the episode with the people of Frome.

The final mention of Frome (p143) is the same rhyme as given in Tongue though in a slightly different version:
>   Rode fete, Beckington rout
>   The devil's in Frome and they can't get him out.

The source here is given as *Wordlore* 1926.

Other Collectors

Berta Lawrence was not an academic folklore researcher. Originally a teacher, she moved to Somerset with her husband in the 1930s and lived near Bridgwater. She wrote many books on the county, and a great deal of poetry, but her main focus was Exmoor and the Quantocks. Her book *Somerset Legends* (1973) is only focused on one aspect of folklore but as there are a few items linked to Frome I have included it.

According to Simpson and Roud (2000) a legend is 'a short traditional oral narrative about a person, place, or object that really exists, existed, or is believed to have existed...' However, much of Lawrence's book reads more like history, albeit dubious, than folklore and most of her material seems to have come from older texts such as Boger (1887). The first section is about saints of importance to the county. Hagiography may be seen as a literary tradition that counted as official history, at least at one time, so it may seem odd to include in folklore at all.

However, though it may have begun as the official version of the elites, by being told person to person it can become part of the lore of the folk as well. Our own founding myth of Aldhelm creating Frome in 685CE has become a well-known story but the historical evidence is scarce. It is also very similar to the founding myths of Bruton, Malmesbury, Bradford-on-Avon and Bishopstrow in Wiltshire.

Lawrence discusses St Aldhelm on pages 32 to 43. The familiar elements are all here; his connection to King Ina, the 'savages' of Selwood/Coit Maur, his habit of attracting converts by singing and playing music on the bridge (or ford) over the local river and the planting of his ash staff that miraculously takes roots and flowers. The turn of Frome comes on pp 36 to 37, with the date given as around 680, when he and six monks arrived here on Midsummer Eve, that is the day before the feast of St John the Baptist himself. There is also extra detail such as the sins of the wicked of Woodlands being badger-baiting and cock-fighting. Lawrence has Aldhelm standing on a little wooden bridge at the southern end of Frome, whereas most people here would say he sat on the banks of the river after crossing the ford where The Bridge is now. She omits the detail of the ash staff, planted wherever Aldhelm planted a church and a common and obvious allegory of his mission. She does use the image of him preaching to pagans, specifically Saxon pagans who worshiped Thor and Woden, though in reality the West Saxons were converted a generation or two earlier.

There are several tales of the miracles of the saint which are not relevant specifically to Frome and a final description of Aldhelm dying at Doulting which links back into folklore in that he was said to be at the house of his unconverted uncle Kenred, believed by some to be the real source of the name Cannards Grave. There is mention of Frome as the first stop on the route of his funeral procession back to Malmesbury.

Frome is also mentioned as the death place of King Edred on page 50 but that is simply history and has no legendary or folkloric aspects. Finally, there is a story about the aftermath of the Monmouth Rebellion in 1685 (p 125) which does link to this town. This is a fairly common tale of a woman or girl going to the officer in charge, often Colonel Kirke himself, and begging for the life of her father, husband, lover or brother. The usual variant is a tale of exploitation, the woman spends the night with the officer but the man or boy she was trying to save is executed anyway. A slightly softer version has a young girl charming the officer with her innocent pleas but her brother/father being accidentally executed despite the order to release him. It is a variant of the latter that interests us here as the twelve-year-old who begs for the life of her brother in Taunton's *White Hart* is none other than our own Elizabeth Singer Rowe. Her age is correct for that year, and she and her family may have been in Taunton around the right time. So far so convincing and if this snippet is true it is not folklore but, rather brutal, history. However, there is absolutely no evidence for Mrs Rowe having a brother. It would appear that the name of the famous poetess has been inserted into a well-known tale. Legends and tales have details changed as they move. In many cases this would allow us to pinpoint where the version originated but she was so well-known that in truth this could probably have come from anywhere between here and Taunton.

It does however attest to the popularity of these tales and her own fame that she should have been given a part in a folktale like this. Lawrence does not cite her sources however Boger's *Myths, Scenes & Worthies of Somerset* is listed in her bibliography and this tale can be found on page 584 of that book, though the individual to be saved is not named specifically as her brother but a 'friend'. If anything, this renders it even less convincing and suggests someone was trying to put her famous name into the story but found it difficult to find an appropriate male connection given her young age and known piety. The tale type in general is referenced, and dismissed as fiction, by Allan Fea in *King Monmouth* (1902, p 382).

I have already mentioned Poole's *The Customs, Superstitions, and Legends of the County of Somerset* (1877). This book was probably the earliest attempt to study the folklore of the county in its own right, rather than as interesting asides in books on other subjects such as histories or travel guides. It has clearly been the source for many later writers with Tongue, Palmer and Lawrence relying heavily on it. However, as well as a great deal of classical myth given for comparison, much of the Somerset material is literary rather than from true folk tradition, being taken from older writings. For the rest very, few sources are given and many of the beliefs are simply summarized as being held in the county as a whole in a general 'people believe' manner, rather than offering any proof or quotes. There is not a single mention of Frome and Shepton Mallet is once again the nearest place cited.

1992 Ray Gibbs' book *Somerset Places & Legends* is another book that is rather misnamed, being about 20 places around Glastonbury with Pilton the closest to Frome. Gibbs was known for his work on the Glastonbury legends so this is not surprising and perhaps 'Mid-Somerset Places & Legends' just didn't have the same ring to it.

Alan Holt was again not a folklore researcher as such, but a retired vicar known for his guides to driving tours around the county's less-frequented areas, with interesting titbits of the 'weird, uncanny and strange' about each of the villages along the way. His book *Folklore of Somerset* (1992) was a collection of these. Strictly speaking, many of the incidents would not count as folklore at all, being bizarre historical facts and reports of murders and mysteries rather than oral traditions. Apart from an account of the ghostly rider sometimes seen in Nunney on pages 112-15, there is one item of interest to us here, the tale of the 'false death' of Edmund Leversedge (pp 57-60). Most of the details of the history given here are simply wrong, including the dates (by at least 80 years), the family relationships and the later history of the manor. Sadly, the author does not give any sources at all so it is impossible to trace his version further. This is an item of folklore from Frome that is truly fascinating as it is a rare case where we have a few scraps of actual history, a physical object in the cadaver tomb in St John's, Edmund's own writing on the subject as well as several versions of the story over the years. It is a tale that has been kept alive and is still re-told locally so it is interesting that this is the only book I surveyed that included it.

Sharon Jacksties' book *Somerset Folk Tales* (2012) was part of a huge series by The History Press. Every county in Britain and Ireland has its own volume of tales, written specifically by storytellers rather than academic folklorists with the intention that the legends and folk tales would be rediscovered and retold, rather than trying to trace the history of folkloric belief. This led to a rather uneven quality overall but our county was well served by Sharon's re-tellings. However, she arranged the tales by landscape type such as coastal areas, moorland and so on, rather than district, and few sources are given. It is therefore difficult to judge whether any of the tales are from this part of the county. In a private communication she confirmed that she found little in the eastern part of the county at all and nothing from Frome. She believes that collectors would be attracted to more remote rural regions, rather than industrial centres.

Conclusion

On beginning this survey, I was aware that there was not much to be found specifically on Frome in the classic, Somerset-wide collections of folklore. I had assumed this was because the many collectors simply ignored this area, probably in a romantic search for an authentic rustic tradition that was unlikely to be found in an industrial town. However, it would seem that despite the titles with 'Somerset' in them, all of the collectors were really focused on a small part of the county to begin with, with the eastern part the least visited. Having said that, most collectors did not conduct any original collecting themselves directly from informants, instead plundering the same older sources again and again. There were actually more snippets of lore, rather than complete narrative, than I expected. It should also be remembered that some of the beliefs, celebrations and so on found elsewhere in Somerset and in Wiltshire would have been found here too, if only someone had come and asked.

In the second part of this article I will move on to other sources such as newspapers and journals, published diaries, place names and court cases which will hopefully give a fuller picture of the folklore heritage of Frome and provide a basis for any future collecting in the area. It is also possible that further research has been done but not yet published. Whatever is found will inform heritage work in the preservation and communication of the unique culture of this town. Folklore is not a moment in time caught in a single snapshot of the past long gone. It is a continuous process of creating and sharing the knowledge that is held by living communities. I have already found a great deal more about traditional beliefs and knowledge in the town but that, as we storytellers say, is a story for another time.

Works Cited

Boger, Charlotte Gilson Allen, *Myths, Scenes & Worthies of Somerset,* George Redway, London, 1887

Cuming Walters, John, *Bygone Somerset,* W. Andrews, London, 1897

Davis, Mick, *Of Mounds and Men: Prehistoric Barrows of the Frome Area,* Frome Society for Local Study, Frome, 2020.

Farbrother, John E., *Shepton Mallet: Notes on its History, ancient, descriptive, and natural,* Albert Byrt, Shepton Mallet, 1872 via archive.org

Fea, Allan, *King Monmouth, being a history of the career of James Scott, "the Protestant Duke", 1649-1685*, J Lane, London, 1902

Gibbs, Ray, *Somerset Places & Legends*, Llanerch Publishers, Felinfach, 1992

Jacksties, Sharon, *Somerset Folk Tales,* The History Press, Stroud, 2012.

Harte, Jeremy, *Cloven Country: The Devil and the English Landscape*, Reaktion Books, London, 2022

Holt, Alan, *Folklore of Somerset*, Alan Sutton Publishing, Stroud, 1992

Lawrence, Berta, *Somerset Legends,* David & Charles, Newton Abbot, 1973.

Massey, George, *The Bells of Frome Deanery,* Frome 1300 Publications, Frome, 1985.

Palmer, Kingsley, *Oral Folk-Tales of Wessex,* David & Charles, Newton Abbot, 1973.

Palmer, Kingsley, *The Folklore of Somerset*, Batsford, London, 1976

Pickering, Andrew, *The Witches of Selwood,* The Hobnob Press, Gloucester, 2021.

Poole, Charles Henry, *The Customs, Superstitions, and Legends of the County of Somerset,* Sampson Low, Marston, Searle and Rivington, London, 1877.

Readers Digest Association, *Folklore, Myths and Legends of Britain,* Readers Digest London, 1973

Simpson, Jacqueline and Roud, Steve, *A Dictionary of English Folklore,* Oxford University Press, 2000.

Tongue, Ruth, 'Some Notes on Modern Somerset Witch-Lore, in *Folklore* 1963, Vol. 74 No 1 pp 321-25

Tongue, Ruth, *Somerset Folklore: County Folklore Vol. VIII,* The Folk-lore Society, London, 1965.

Tongue, Ruth, *The Chime Child or Somerset Singers,* Routledge & Kegan Paul Ltd, London, 1968.

Westwood, Jennifer and Simpson, Jacqueline, *The Lore of the Land: A Guide to England's Legends, from Spring-Heeled Jack to the Witches of Warboys,* Penguin Books, London, 2005.

FROME BUILDINGS 26: MERCHANT'S BARTON HOUSE

A Challenge in Logistics & Restoration

Terrie Riera,

This article, first appeared in *Guardian Angel* newsletter of the Bradford on Avon Preservation Trust, Issue 41 Summer of 2003 and is reproduced with their kind permission.

To look at the magnificent 17th century carved plaster ceiling in Priory Barn Cottage, Newtown today, one could well think that it is in the room for which it was made. Resplendent with its centre rosette and patterned surround of teasels, Tudor roses, thistles and fleur de lys bespeaking its English wool town origins in the 17th century – it looks comfortably situated and very much at home, framed beautifully by a frieze of perhaps slightly later date.

The rear of Merchant's Barton by Eunice Overend c.1936

But indeed it is the frieze, bearing the mark 1658 with the initials 'JM' and 'HM' that more clearly identifies the owners of the original house from which it came, Merchant's Barton House in Frome, home of a Frome clothier, Henry Merchant and his wife Joan from about 1658 to 1696, but also remembered as a nice little stationery shop on Church Street from about WWI times, or more recently, by the area's industrial estate which took the same name. Sadly, the house fell subject to demolition in 1970 and is now the entrance to Saxon Vale.

The fact that this beautiful ceiling survived such fate is now the subject of a near legendary tale involving the celebrated instincts, skill and determination of Elizabeth Stephenson, the highly regarded co-founder of the Bradford on Avon Preservation Trust. For, as indicated in John Teed's article in the *Guardian Angel* of autumn 1993, 'At the time when restoration was starting on converting Priory Barn, Elizabeth was driving through Frome and saw a very good 17th century building with bulldozes waiting to start demolition. She went in and saw a very good 17th century ceiling in one of the rooms." She managed to halt the demolition and, then serving as chairman of the trust, got permission to take the ceiling, which was purchased by the trust for the grand sum of £500.

Five hundred pounds may seem remarkable price to look at it today, but the ceiling was then broken and battered. Just how then, does one move a somewhat dilapidated 17th century ceiling from Frome to Bradford on Avon, reinstating it and restoring it to its original grandeur in the same process? According to Ron Simpson, a member of the trust, and the overall contractor in charge of the bulk of the renovation of Prior Barn Cottage there were several steps involved in the transformation:

Dismantling

Working under the overall direction of Elizabeth Stephenson and Miss MacKean, cofounders of the trust, the specialist ornamental plasterers Moran & Wheatley were retained to dismantle the ceiling in Frome. Basically, they cut it down in squares approximately 3' x 3'-working slowly and carefully as it was in a very fragile condition and quite difficult to saw and lift out - and then transported the squares back to their workshop on the floor of their fully padded van.

Strengthening

Once back at the workshop, Moran & Wheatley strengthened the panels with additional, new timber laths, (or timber strips), hessian reinforcement and additional plaster, basically floating a new layer over the back of the original slab to make it firm.

Restoration's First Phase

Next came the challenging task of carving and restoring the design and surface on the panels to a suitable state for refitting, which involved a considerable amount of very talented work from the carvers, Ted Pegram and Chris Short, (the latter of whom is still with the firm today)

Removal and Storage

The sections were then stored for over a year by John Teed.

Preparations at Priory Barn Cottage

About this time, working with the builder, Jack Mizen, efforts had been completed on the first phase of the restoration of Priory Barn from an original untouched barn to a configuration involving the present suite of meeting rooms and support areas on the left, together with a shell with windows and openings on the right side that was subsequently to become the domestic half of Priory Barn or Priory Barn Cottage. As soon as funds were available for phase two work was ready to commence on the completion of the Cottage and the job, including the walls, plastering, doors, and ceiling, was awarded to Ron Simpson then of Trowbridge Road, Bradford on Avon.

Installation and restoration at Priory Barn Cottage:

As overall contractor and director in charge of the project, Ron and his team first installed a heavy first floor joist and steel beam to take the weight and Moran & Wheatley were appointed as specialist nominated sub-contractors for the work involving the ceiling.

Eric Moran and an assistant fill the gaps.

In fact, Eric Moran, one of the partners in the firm, worked on the ceiling himself together with the carvers, Ted Pegram and Chris Short.

During this stage the ceiling was cut to 16 feet by 18.5 feet to fit the size of the room then nailed up in sections and screwed or nailed to the joists. Once in position the gaps between the sections were caulked with hessian, which stops them from cracking, and filled with plaster. The cornice was then completely re-made using a cast from an original section that was still in good order when found at Merchants Barton House in Frome, (and this mould still remains at Moran and Wheatley today). As a result of this process the majority of the ceiling that one sees today is original. However, some portions, understandably, had to be re-carved and restored, but as to which is original and which is restored, it is very difficult to see – a great credit to all the very talented artisans involved.

Ron, in fact remembers the work to be meticulous and of the highest standard indeed. "I know on one occasion, the other partner, Albert Wheatley, came on the site, parked his Rolls-Royce outside, and dressed as always immaculately in his business suit, inspected the work in progress, feeling uneasy about some of the panels. He then proceeded to commence work himself, still beautifully dressed and left the site by 4.30 as white as the ceiling he was erecting. After I commented on it, he said, 'It's alright. It will go back to the cleaners tomorrow and come back perfect. It has happened before'".

By 21 July 1972, the ceiling was finished at the subject of a feature article in the *Wiltshire Times and News* entitled, "Preservation Trust saves 17th Century Ceiling" with much thanks to Miss Stephenson's insights and determination, Miss MacKean's dedicated watchful eye, and the Bradford on Avon Preservation Trust, Moran and Wheatley, Ron's exacting standards of professionalism and the fine team of artisans involved. Now recently redecorated using the specialist paints of the period, it is very much a treasure of Bradford on Avon and definitely a joy to see.

* There is a photograph in Frome Yearbook 19 p.78

THE GEORGE INN, NORTON ST PHILLIP

John E Chard

The George Inn lies in the lovely Somerset village of Norton St Phillip and is deservedly one of the best-known pubs in the country as well almost certainly one of the oldest. It is believed to have first been granted a licence as an inn in 1397 to accommodate travellers coming to the fair the charter for which was first granted in 1255.

THE GEORGE INN, NORTON ST. PHILIP. THE OLDEST LICENSED INN IN ENGLAND. BUILT 1223—LICENSED 1397

SIDE VIEW OF THE GEORGE INN, SHOWING ITS GOTHIC DOORWAY

There is an excellent article on its history and architecture in Volume 18 of the Frome Yearbook for 2015 obtainable as a free download from the museum website. This interesting set of ten sepia photographs was produced by The Regal Art Publishing Company who began publishing postcards in 1906 under the proprietorship of Albert Cox, 28, Upper George Street, London.

FRONT DOOR OF THE GEORGE INN, NORTON ST. PHILIP

COURTYARD OF THE OLD GEORGE INN, SHOWING THE TURRET WITH THE OCTAGONAL STAIR CASE, ALSO THE BALCONY WHERE JUDGE JEFFERIES MADE HIS COURT AFTER THE MONMOUTH REBELLION

THE GOTHIC DOORWAY LEADING TO THE COURTYARD

BAR OF THE GEORGE INN, NORTON ST. PHILIP

Cox specialised in sets of picturesque county views. The ten cards reproduced here were commissioned by John Edgar Chard a former stone mason who took over from Arthur Crook as landlord with his wife Ada in April 1916 at the age of 31.During that year he successfully applied to a tribunal for exemption from military service. He was a popular licensee at the George for 22 years until 1938 when he moved across the road to run the Fleur de Lis (sic) until his death in 1946.

THE RECEPTION ROOMS OF THE MONKS, SHOWING THE OAK PANELLING

TAP ROOM OF THE GEORGE INN, WHICH THE MONKS MADE THEIR KITCHEN

The *North Wilts Herald* for 22 September 1933 has a long account of its reporter being taken on a guided tour by Chard, described as 'white haired and jovial' and 'knowing, 'every nook and cranny of the rambling old building ' still lit by oil lamps as 'electricity has not yet come to Norton'.

THE ROOM WHICH THE DUKE OF MONMOUTH OCCUPIED BEFORE THE BATTLE OF SEDGEMOOR, ON THE 26 JUNE, 1685, WHEN AN ATTEMPT WAS MADE TO SHOOT HIM, AS HE STOOD AT THE WINDOW

THE UPPER ROOM OF THE GEORGE INN, WHERE THE BROAD-CLOTH MERCHANTS MADE THEIR SALES OF WOOL

Very little has changed over the years and it is a shame that we are unable date them more closely. In an interesting link to Frome the shot of the bar has a framed advertisement for Mansford & Baily, Frome, behind the bar, otherwise known as the Wheatsheaf in Bath Street, now the popular music venue known simply by its address, '23 Bath Street'.

I have added one more card which is not from the Chard series but from the same period and shows one of the locals enjoying a mug of cider and smoking his pipe. To the left of the picture partly obscured by the label is a bagatelle table seldom seen today but very popular in pubs before the war when it was usurped by bar billiards now itself replaced by American pool.

The Tap Room. Note the bagatelle table on the left

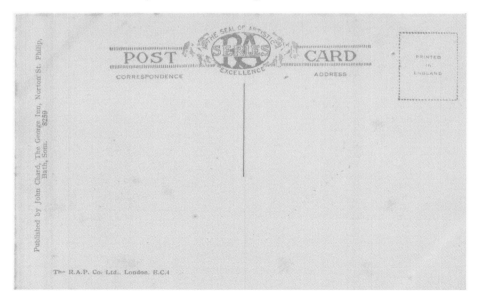

The set has now been donated to Frome Museum under acc. no P4583

Not many people know this, but there is a team of very small posties who work secretly through the night to bring us our mail. They have to be small enough to get through the letterbox and fish out items for delivery. These two seem to have fallen asleep at Welshmill. They were there when I walked into town early one morning but by the time I returned they had gone.

Passerby

THE FROME LITERARY INSTITUTION 1845

Derek Gill

The following article by local historian Derek Gill first appeared in the *Frome Journal* for 20 August 1981.

The Frome Literary and Scientific Institution was founded in 1844. It could have been established 30 years earlier for at the annual meeting of the Frome Reading Society, on the 25 March 1814, a Literary Institute was proposed, and largely supported by one who could later claim to be the father of the 'Lit', Thomas Bunn. On that occasion, and again in 1836 the idea failed to gain enough support and it was not until 1843 that the suggestion was again made. Thomas Green of South Parade who kept a diary, now in Frome Museum, wrote,

January 23, 1843

'Attended a meeting at the Vicarage, (Saint John's) for establishing a lecture room and museum, present Messrs. Dusautoy, Meade, Jones, G Sheppard, B Sheppard, John Sheppard and myself. After some discussion it was agreed to make a commencement and Mr John Sheppard promised to give £10 and Mr George Sheppard and myself £5 each if £200 were raised besides an annual 20 shillings.'

In those days few bought daily newspapers, the only source of national and international news were the London papers which cost 5d, apart from The Times, which, with the largest circulation was 7d. At that time there was a stamp duty and no reduction in the price of papers could be made until its abolition in 1855. A reading room as was envisaged, would enable more people to read a newspaper. One of the first priorities was to find suitable premises. Thomas Green continued,

January 30 1843

'Attended a meeting at the Vicarage on the proposed Library and Lecture Rooms and went with Mr J Sheppard to look at two houses in Bath Street'.

October 16, 1844

'Met Messers Dusautoy, Daniel and Giles at the house in Bath Street and Vicarage Street to ascertain the best suited for the library'.

Eventually the Masonic Hall in Palmer Street next to the present Old Bath Arms was chosen and served the Society for over 20 years. In February 1843 Thomas Bunn had called a meeting inviting steps to be taken for the establishment of such a society. A letter had been printed and circulated inviting members and dated 1 February at Frome Vicarage, it read,

'It has been thought desirable that some measures be taken to promote the union and communications for literary and scientific purposes amongst the inhabitants of Frome and its neighbourhood: that it would be, therefore, expedient to commence the formation of a library, and to hire apartments, where books and other collections may be kept, and used, as well as to obtain from members of the proposed Society or from others, occasional literary and scientific lectures. Donations and subscriptions with some gifts of books, have already been promised and will be received by the Rev. WSO Dusautoy (curate of Frome in the permanent absence of the vicar), the Rev. RJ Meade, (vicar of Christ Church) Mr John Sheppard, (of Iron Gates) and the two Frome banks where the copy of the rules agreed may be inspected'.

17 people gave their names to this appeal headed by Thomas Bunn who was then in his late 70s.

The Institute was to be managed by committee including a president, vice president, treasurer, secretary and other members. A subscription of not under 10 shillings was to constitute a member, whilst one guinea admitted a member to the private reading room for a year. There was to be no religious or political controversy. The rooms were to be open from 10 am until 9 pm daily except Sundays.

Amongst the first members were most of the local leading citizens and clergy, Nonconformist and Anglican. However, there was controversy in 1853 when the Roman Catholic priest Fr Ward applied to join. Only two members supported him and they resigned in protest at this intolerance. Initially 110 people joined the society. A programme of lectures on travel, natural science, philosophy and other classics was prepared, occasionally, a paid lecturer was to be booked for variety. On January 24 1845 the inaugural lecture was given by the Rev. Richard Meade, Thomas Green wrote of the occasion,

'Attended introductory lecture of the Frome Literary Institute at the George Assembly Rooms, delivered by Mr Meade at 7 o'clock. The room was full and the lecture admirable. Mr John Sheppard made a good extempore speech afterwards, as did Mr Horner of Wells, the president, Mr Dusautoy proposed that Mr Meade's address be published'.

The society became a centre for most of Frome society and did more than any other institution to promote the social and intellectual progress of the town, and immediately became the most popular according to contemporary witnesses. Over 600 visited it in its first year. Some of the members who had wandered to all parts of the world sent back interesting communications. Many prominent citizens of Frome donated items to the society, among these the Rev John Horner of Mells gave 253 books and a collection of minerals, corals, shells, insects and fossils as well as 100 cases of birds and two cabinets of medals and coins.

Of these Thomas Green wrote:

19 February 1845

'To Mells Park to look at the cabinets and a glass cases given by Mr Horner to the Literary Institute which far exceeded our expectations.'

6 March 1845

'Went with J Daniel to Mells Park where we were engaged till evening and packing up the minerals presented by Mr Horner to the Literary Institute. Returned to tea and then went back to the rooms and put away what we brought home'.

22 March 1845

'Accompanied JE Daniel to Mells where we packed up the remaining drawers of minerals and dined with Mr Raines'.

John Sheppard gave 108 books, Mr Wickham of North Hill House gave 90 books, and Thomas Bunn a set of Chippendale chairs and 14 objects for the museum. In fact, the latter was far more generous. He bequeathed all his pictures and objects of art. Shortly before his death he executed a deed of gift of Monmouth House and other property which he hoped would enable the society to build permanent premises on the southside of Christchurch Street West opposite Rook Lane House, where he envisaged a grand crescent to rival Bath.

His 'Temple of Science', the centre of the crescent, was to be the premises of the Institute and would have been a real architectural ornament to the town standing in such a prominent position. Unfortunately, his gift was so complicated in its conception that after his death his trustees were unable to proceed with it. A perusal of the wealth of books in the library of the Institute shows the breadth of vision and interest of those early members. Many bear the surnames, Sheppard, Bunn, Horner and other leading families of the time. One I examined recently originally belonged to Mrs Elizabeth Rowe, poet who lived in Rook Lane House until her death in 1736. The flyleaf records her gift of the book to Eleanor Sheppard and successive Sheppard owners until the last, John, who gave it to the 'Lit'.[1]

At the inaugural meeting of the Institute, the President of the Royal Society, the Marquess of Northampton, was made patron and the Rev JSH Horner, rector of Mells, was elected president. The vice presidents were John Sheppard, Dr JS Harrison, the Rev WS Dusautoy, the Rev RJ Meade, Mr James Wickham, (a local solicitor), and Alfred Whitaker (another solicitor). The Rev Alfred Daniel vicar of Holy Trinity, was chosen as first librarian and Thomas Bunn, then aged 76 the first secretary. In the 1860s the Earl of Cork and Orrery of Marston House was president and Thomas Green treasurer.

By the 1860s the society had outgrown its first premises and a long struggle followed to find more permanent ones. Thomas Bunn's dream never materialised and it was thanks to the generosity of a local cloth manufacturer, John Sinkins, of Wallbridge House that a final solution was found. He financed the building which now graces the corner of Bridge Street and North Parade at a cost of several thousand pounds. It was designed by a relative, Thomas Hine of Plymouth and was built by Carr and Pickford. To commemorate his gift his initials and arms were placed above the front door. The Institute therefore, finally acquired spacious premises which provided a fine reading room, museum and a flat for the caretaker.

At the annual meeting on 8 October 1869 members spoke in glowing terms of their new premises. John Sinkins died shortly before, but he had lived to see his creation completed. At that time there were 3,197 books listed in society's catalogue with 107 members. Now, over a century later there is the exciting prospect that the building will once again fill the purpose for which it was conceived. It is hoped that very shortly, Frome Museum, now in cramped conditions at Wine Street House will move to the 'Lit'. This is a natural marriage which will once again bring life to the old building and restore it to a life of education and research, housing the increasing amount of local records being acquired by the museum, but also be a centre where residents and visitors may study the history of Frome and its industries.

The institution's inaugural lecture.

The Frome Literary and Scientific Institution held its inaugural lecture on 24 January 1845 at the Assembly Room linked to The George Hotel. The room, above the market hall, opened in 1818 and paid for by Lord Cork;[2] was until recently occupied by the NatWest Bank.

The Assembly Room at the George in 1906. Top floor on the far left.

Between January and April of that year 13 lectures were given and published in book form, edited by Rev. RJ Meade vicar of Christchurch in Frome and printed by WP Penny of Bath Street[3] Amongst talks on Waterloo, Palestine and the Political Constitution of the Ancient States, was one on Geology by Rev Charles J Middleditch who was vicar of Badcox Lane Baptist Church from 1837-1856. He is responsible for the disfiguring mass of Doric frontage to his church in Catherine Street which was completed in 1846 but despite this it seems that he was well liked and took part in many community activities.

His lecture is reproduced here. (He begins by praising the previous speaker whose lecture is not recorded.)

Geology

'Whatever favourable opinion was previously entertained, the lecture has exceeded, I believe, everyone's expectation, by the extent of knowledge, the cleverness of expression, and the tact with which the speaker has made so difficult a topic clear to the understanding of some of us who are unlearned. One of our naval friends has happily illustrated the learned observations drawn from books, by his beautiful description of the natural wonders which came under his immediate observation at the distance of the antipodes, and by comparing the scenes in that distant region with more fascinating charms at home. I think he spoke of coral beds of the astonishing length of 800 miles which are not to be visited without danger, and near which, I believe the French ships, equipped for Maritime discovery, and commanded by Admiral Peyrouse, were lost.

Rev Charles Middleditch

Perhaps it may not be uninteresting if I notice some of the geological appearances nearer home. Many years ago, the Marquess of Bath, the grandfather of the present Marquess, expended about one hundred thousand pounds, under the guidance of Sir Jeffrey Wyattville, in the improvement of his ancient mansion. among other things it was determined to sink the fine piece of water near it to a lower level, and the excavator brought me a beautiful fossil nautilus, found six or eight feet below the bed of the original lake.

When we excavated Bath Street, more than 30 years ago, we found pieces of wood imbedded in stone, as hard as marble. I took a stone in my hand from a wall in one of my own fields, a few days since and it was replete with fossil sea shells. I know that modern philosophers tell a different tale; but I have little faith in their opinions, and it appears to me perfectly probable that these transitions from the sea to the land happened at the period of the deluge.

We have in this parish inexhaustible stores of building stone, tiles, and paving stone, with the plain mark, as one of our friends has observed, of the ripple of water on the surface before it has attained hardness. I mention this partly, because our vanity leads us to send to a distance for blue pavement, which is more pleasing to the eye, but not so suitable to our hills. The smooth pavement is slippery in winter, and leads some of our neighbours to try a geological experiment. They slide, and their animal substance falling, makes a violent assault on the stones which usually support their feet. The mineral substance takes offence, and returns the blow, and as it strikes hardest, usually gains the victory. Then the animal substance, looking much disconcerted, walks limping away, if we were not too vain to use the pavement with a rough surface provided in our quarries, this inconvenience would be prevented.

Oolite, producing lead, which is a novelty in geology, and limestone, approach and mingle with each other.

In ascending from the Market-place to Keyford, if a well is sunk, it is 70 feet deep. At the highest point at Keyford, the water rises by a natural spring on the surface and sometimes flows over. On the other side of the hill it is necessary to sink 100 feet deep to obtain water.

A relation of mine, joined with others to sink a pit for coal at Clan Down, in this neighbourhood. They expended £10,500, and, not finding coal in their pit, sold the adventure for £1,500. The purchasers, aware that the cutting had passed through a fault, opened some lateral passages, soon found coal, and it became, and still is, one of the most profitable mines, producing yearly, thousands. A little more knowledge of geology would have placed the profits in the pockets of the first proprietors.

In the same neighbourhood, some miners, finding it a troublesome task to draw little waggons of coal in avenues at the bottom of the pit, lowered an ass to assist them; but the newcomer had no taste for geological pursuits underground. Neither persuasion nor blows could induce him to work. After a week's stay he was drawn up, and when he found himself again in a pasture field, with the sun shining upon his long ears, he set up a bray louder, if not sweeter, then the voice of a nightingale, and galloped through the country, over the hedge and a ditch, for a mile, to testify his joy. I have more respect for the sagacity of this animal, who rejoiced in the light of the sun, then for the class of geologists who array the works of the Creator against the words of the God of truth. I have no desire to partake of the desolation of mind and heart which must find and overtake those who forget,God, or rebel against him, or deny his holy word. However unworthy, I had rather partake of the feelings of my respected Father, who, being on his death bed was requested by an affectionate friend, to endeavour to compose himself to sleep. He answered –"No! I had rather employ my time in thinking of the myriad of Saints and Angels whom I hope soon to join."

Foreign marbles are commonly used; but I have collected a variety of specimens from England and Wales and Scotland and Ireland, some of them as beautiful as those from abroad. They are sold at about half the price but are harder. Scotch Mineralogists state that their country produces fine statuary marble; but I never could obtain any, *and I doubt* whether it exists.

A Museum of economic Geology has been established by Government under the direction of Sir Henry De La Beche, containing specimens illustrative of the application of geology to the useful purposes of Life. The value of the subterranean riches of Great Britain amounts annually to upwards of twenty millions. This Museum is open to the public gratis, and, though chiefly arranged for useful purposes, contains some specimens of great beauty.

The Airdrie estate has recently produced to its proprietor, Sir W Alexander, a clear income of £12,000 yearly, for blackband iron-stone alone, where not one shilling of mineral rent was formally received. The discovery of its value was at first treated with indifference and neglect, instead of being acknowledged as a public benefactor.

The ancestor of a friend of mine was so fortunate as to possess a small mineral of great value, the Pit diamond. He sold it for a very large sum to the French King of that period, who paid for it by instalments. The king wore it as a button on his hat. My friend lately showed me a copy in glass of the exact dimension, and now enjoys a considerable estate at Maiden Bradley, purchased with part of the produce of the Diamond.

I have not heard the Museum of Cuvier mentioned in this room, which, if I am rightly informed, must be the most curious in the world, consisting wholly of the skeletons of animals who have disappeared from the earth, and have ceased to exist.

Our government has for centuries sent out the voyagers towards the north pole, where nothing has been, or will be found, except ice and snow; and adventurers frequently visit the unhealthy climate of Africa, while the immense country of Australia blessed with the finest climate in the world, and in our own peaceable possession, remains almost unexplored. A single regiment of soldiers dispersed in small forts, accompanied by scientific men well versed in the best mode of supplying Artesian wells, would soon discover all treasures, - vegetable, animal, and mineral, which are contained in a country larger than Europe.

It will be pleasing to the Members of the Society to learn that the Rev. Lecturer on Geology is willing to give a Lecture in the next Session, "On the Harmony of Geology with Revelation." This requires extreme knowledge of the subject, great reverence for the Scriptures, and so much judgement in the exposition and application of these topics, that it will be difficult to find another person whose competence and discretion it could be so safely intrusted.'

[1] It is most unfortunate that before handing ownership over to the museum the Literary Institute decided to auction off the contents of his own museum and there was a major sale which took place on the 12th of June 1981 although much had been disappearing since the early 70s. Many items had been on loan rather than directly owned by the Institute but it seems that no records were kept and today nothing remains of what must have been magnificent collection. See Frome Preserved: A Museum's History. by Dr David Robinson 2016

[2] Cork lived at Marston House within the grounds of Marston Bigot Park. He employed architect Jeffry Wyattville in 1817 to embellish the central block with four Ionic columns. Wyattville was known locally for his work at Longleat and then at the Church of St John in the same decade. In 1821, on the corner of the then named Hill Street and the Market Place in Frome, the Earl was persuaded by Thomas Bunn to build an Assembly Room above a covered market, in the style of the Greek revival; in 1822, the street was renamed Cork Street. He had been shown by Bunn an image of the Roman Forum as 'a good design for a modern market-place'; Cork demurred and 'thought of economy and said it would not pay'. Bunn's persuasion paid off; it remains one of Frome's notable buildings, now a bank with the ground floor enclosed. They worked together on various other projects, including the National and Christ Church Schools, with the Earl as the chair of committee. The Earl contributed to local charities such as the Blanket Fund and the Coal Fund, both for the relief of the poor, and chaired meetings of the Frome Savings Bank.

[3] Thanks to Glynis Tingay for bringing this book to my attention. The original now resides in Frome Museum and may be downloaded in PDF form from their website. This is probably the only surviving copy. The British Library were sent a copy in digital format but declined to accept it.

FROME'S CARDING

Jon Stean

In 1720 Daniel Defoe wrote that *'Frome is now reckoned to have more people in it, than the city of Bath, and some say, than even Salisbury itself, and if their trade continues to increase for a few years more, as it has done for those past, it is very likely to be one of the greatest and wealthiest inland towns in England*[1.]

Frome was renowned for the production of excellent woollen broadcloth, but to weave such fine cloth required a lot of preparation. The fleece had to be sorted for the best quality, then washed, the locks had to be separated, dyed, oiled and then carded before spinning a suitably strong thread for the warp and a lofty one for the weft. The 30m warp of up to several thousand threads was then chained and sized all prior to weaving and the many finishing processes that were then applied. The importance of spinning cannot be underestimated, it would take the work of 8 -12 spinners to supply enough yarn for each weaver to produce a broadcloth. Today, it takes six miles of thread to make just one pair of jeans.

At each stage, specialist workers were either paid by the piece or employed by the clothiers in their workshops and later in the mills. Over the centuries, the entire trade had many ups and downs as wars, inspection costs, taxation and tariffs, along with bans on the import of wool and exports of cloth were all imposed to different effects. Many petitions were raised to enforce or dispute opposing arguments. One such, written in 1710 of which a photocopy is held by the Frome museum piqued my curiosity.

American Combs

When wool is spun it needs to be prepared so that the fibres are positioned correctly. Historically, it was suggested that this might have been done with teasels, bows and combs. In Pompeii, the feltmaker Verecundus in the Via dell'Abbondanza had pictures on the outside of his shop showing textile processes and one of these shows a figure who appears to be combing wool fibres.

Since the sixteenth century in Europe, the hand processing of wool for spinning was usually done in one of two ways – combing or carding. Combing wool was the earlier of the two methods and was done to remove short fibres while aligning the long fibres. It is similar to

combing one's hair so that each hair lies parallel to the other. When spun, the yarn is smoother, more lustrous and stronger, this produces a hard wearing worsted fabric.[2]

Hand carding uses a pair of wooden cards that have rows of wire teeth set into a leather base and glued to a paddle shaped wooden board with a handle. The washed and oiled locks are alternatively transferred from one card to the other as the short fibres are aligned into an airy web and the broken bits and vegetable matter are removed. The web of fibres is then formed into a rolag ready for spinning. Carded fibres produce woollen threads which are loosely woven into a cloth that is then fulled (felted) into a heavy, thick material suitable for outerwear.

German wool carder who died in 1653

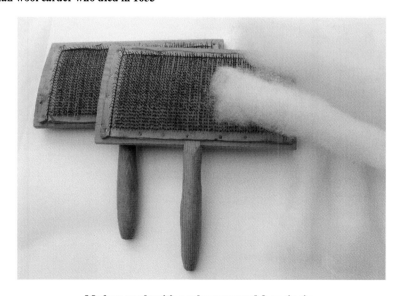

Modern cards with a rolag prepared for spinning

Frome was one of the principal centres of the carding industry and wire drawing was integral to the process of making wool cards which are still used today. This was a cold process that involved pulling metal through a series of successively smaller dies until the cross section reached the desired size for the cards. In 1705, Roger Leversedge granted a plot of waste land at Egford to Thomas Mounshore, a wire drawer of Frome - was this to erect a small workshop for himself and others? Considerable money could also be made as some of Frome's wire drawers left substantial legacies, James Gibbons in 1719, John King in 1737 and Peter Maskell in 1733, whose daughter Joanna was married to a member of the Button family. These were well connected men with numerous properties in Frome and their sons and daughters married into the prominent clothier families of the Whitchurches, Pobjays, and Edgells. One will also mentions Thomas Bunn as executor. The inventory of Thomas Gane card maker in 1674 lists tools, old handles, a bench and cards along with several leases on properties. There is the inventory of Edward Holdway and the wills of card makers James Baber in 1703 and Isaac Rawlings in 1839. The Rawlings factory later produced leather belting before closing in 1972.[3]

In 1710, the Landholders of Frome petitioned Lord Weymouth on behalf of the Wire-drawers, Card-makers and Clothiers of Froome for help in getting Parliament to bring a bill to prevent the selling of old Wool-Cards. This was not a new problem as there was already an Act of Parliament passed during the reign of Charles II. While some were selling old cards, they were actually resetting the old wire into new leather and boards and selling them as new. However, the wire had been weakened by use which affected the quality of the product. They wished Parliament to enforce this Act and to stiffen the penalties. They proposed that the benefits for Froome would be the *"lessening the rates to the poor of the said parish by keeping the greater part thereof imployed in the Manufacture of making the Cards"*[4].

This petition to Lord Weymouth followed a petition delivered to the House of Commons earlier in the year on 29 January 1710. The petition was read to the House; and, a committee of west country MPs was commissioned to produce a Bill for the House's approval. Unlike the lackadaisical approach of the modern House of Commons they were instructed to meet at 'Five a Clock on the same day'. Sir William Windham (more usually known as Sir William Wyndham of Orchard Wyndham near Williton, Somerset) reported for this Committee on 2 February 1710. The Committee stated that, 'the using of good Wool Cards in the making of Cloth, is of great Concernement to the Trade of this Kingdom in the Woollen Manufacture, the Iron Wire of old Cards being too weak, and insufficient, for the well carding of Wool.'[5]

It was resolved that the House be moved for Leave to bring in a Bill for the more effectual preventing the Importation of foreign white wire and the selling of old cards. Again, with a speed unlike our modern Parliament, Sir William presented a 'Bill to prohibit the Importation of foreign Wool Cards, and to prevent the Abuses in making the same with Old Card Wire'. This was received by the House and read the first time and it was resolved that the Bill be read a second time. Similar petitions were presented by the citizens of Trowbridge, Westbury, Bradford (Wilts), and Tavistock amongst others, so the problem was of concern across the South West. The petitions whilst not quite identical would suggest a co-ordinated campaign. There was a counter argument from other Clothiers of Froom (sic)
…that there is a Clause in a Bill depending in the House, to prohibit the Selling of old Wool Cards, That the Petitioners, already labouring under great Difficulties in Trade, are surprized, that so inconsiderable a Number of People, as the Card-makers are, should attempt to lay a farther Weight upon the Clothiers, to the utter Destruction of the whole Woollen Manufacture, to hinder the Clothier from selling his old Wool Cards.[6] There is no record of the Bill passing and becoming an Act, so perhaps the counter-petition worked.

The petition attempted to improve the implementation of the act of Charles II, which refers to previous Acts of Edward IV and Elizabeth. Recital of 3 E.IV. c.4. §1. 39 Eliz. c. 14. § 1 *that many Poor People have been employed in the making of Wire and Wool Cards; that of late Foreign Card Wire and Wool Cards have been imported, and also that Persons have been engaged in making false Wool Cards; and that great Inconveniences have thereby arisen. Foreign Wool Cards or Card Wire, &c. not to be imported; nor false Wool Cards put to sale. Importing, or making and putting to Sale false Wool Cards; Penalty"*[7].

One of the earliest machines of the industrial revolution was the spinning jenny invented in the mid-eighteenth century, but this device improved the efficiency of spinning not carding. The flying shuttle was introduced in the 1730s and this improved the speed of weavers. As part of the trend toward mechanisation, carding was the last of these processes to be successfully industrialised. One of the earliest patent applications in this field was from Henry Allen a clothier of Frome, who, in 1725, petitioned for a grant of Letters Patent for his invention of a machine for *'cleansing, hollowing and mixing all sorts of wool Spanish and English'* [8.] Another patent was registered, in 1809 to *"Joseph Clisila Daniell of Frome, clothier, for improvements in dressing woollen cloth and preparing and using wire cards"*[9]. Unfortunately, I was not able to find a lot of background information on the petitions. Carding, combing and spinning were independent of water power so they could be done anywhere, and it is possible that the majority of women and children in and around Frome prepared wool using hand cards.

Carding was much improved in the seventeenth century due to changes made in the West of England. Finer cards produced finer spinning and therefore finer cloth. About 1685 John Aubrey was told by Samuel Ash that *'the art of spinning is so much improved within these last 40 years that one pound of wool makes twice as much cloth as it did before the Civil War*[10].

Dutch arrivals played a part in improving spinning at the end of the seventeenth and the beginning of the eighteenth centuries. Julia de la Mann notes that they produced better cards and that they were definitely linked to Frome in 1706.[11] The Victoria County History for Wiltshire notes that *a curious little controversy in 1710 between the cardmakers and wiredrawers of Frome and the Spanish clothiers that one of Brewer's Dutchmen was a cardmaker and that cards had been so much improved since his arrival that the illicit import of foreign cards and wire had ceased.*[12] This optimistic view can be countered by the petition that started this article. Today card making is more or less redundant, however in its heyday it contributed enormously to the wealth of Frome and as part of the cloth industry, it has left a lasting legacy in the town's heritage and buildings.

[1] Daniel Defoe - *A Tour Through the Whole Island of Great Britain*
[2] The House Books of the Twelve Brothers - www.nuernberger-hausbuecher.de
[3] Wills and Inventories held at the National Archives in Kew
[4] Journals of the House of Commons. v.16 1708-1711.
[5] ibid
[6] ibid
[7] British History Online from 'Charles II, 1662: An Act against importing of Foreign Wool cards wire or Iron wire.', in Statutes of the Realm: Volume 5, 1628- 80, ed. John Raithby
[8] State Papers in the National Archives
[9] Somerset Heritage Centre
[10] Bodleian. MS. Aubrey, 2, f. 64. also from British History Online
[11] Julia de la Mann *The Cloth Industry in the West Country from 1640 to 1880*
[12] 'Textile industries since 1550', in *A History of the County of Wiltshire:* Volume 4, ed. Elizabeth Crittall (London, 1959), pp 148-182. British History Onlin

THOMAS PROWSE OF BERKLEY HOUSE & COMPTON BISHOP

Three Portraits

Penny Gay & David Crellin

In 1988 a very fine article about Berkley House, near Frome, written by the late architectural historian Giles Worsley, appeared in *Country Life* magazine.[1] It included a black and white photograph of a portrait in a Rococo frame, proudly displayed in the hall at Berkley. The gentleman in the portrait was identified as Thomas Prowse (1708 – 1767), former Lord of the Manor of Berkley, a highly respected MP and an eminent amateur architect. A very similar image of this same portrait, reproduced below, was discovered in the research file of art historian, Evelyn Newby.[2] Prowse is pictured holding an architect's dividers in his right hand and appears to have been drawing a circular plan. Clearly in this painting he has been portrayed as an acknowledged gentleman architect.

A coloured image of a portrait owned by Axbridge Town Trust and also known to be of Thomas Prowse can be found on the website artuk.org. It is pictured without its frame, but the painting itself looks to be almost identical to the one displayed in the Hall at Berkley House, the only obvious difference being that the sitter is holding nothing in his right hand and there is no architectural drawing. Instead, we see Thomas Prowse in his role as a long-standing and greatly valued M.P. His hands rest on the pages of a book of Parliamentary Bills placed open on the table in front of him. This portrait and also the book depicted in it were among the gifts donated to Axbridge Town Trust from the Prowse Estate.[3]

Both portraits were almost certainly by the same artist – and probably commissioned at about the same time (now thought to have been the late 1750s) – but why were they almost identical, yet noticeably different? Further background information about the life and career of Thomas Prowse may well provide an explanation.

Monochrome Image of a Portrait at Berkley House, Frome. Paul Mellon Centre for Studies in British Art

Thomas Prowse, Esquire was a gentleman worthy of far greater attention than the scope of this particular article allows. Baptised in London in 1708, Thomas was the grandson of John Prowse, a descendant of a minor gentry family from Devon, and would eventually inherit Berkley House in Somerset, which had come into the possession of the Prowse family following the marriage of his paternal grandfather to Anne Newborough in 1670. In that same year, following the death of an uncle, William Prowse, John also inherited a fine seventeenth century house at Compton Bishop, near Axbridge. Thomas's father another John, inherited both houses, but, after his early death from smallpox in 1710, when Thomas was only two, his wife Abigail spent much of her long widowhood at Berkley, often joined by her father George Hooper, Bishop of Bath and Wells.[4]

Following her father's death in 1727, Abigail Prowse commissioned Nathaniel Ireson, architect and builder, to take down the old house at Berkley and build a new one in the Palladian style. It is clear from her precise instructions and comments to Ireson that the house was to be exactly as she wanted, down to the finest details. Building would have been under way when her son Thomas married in London in 1731 and the house was completed in 1732.[5]

Berkley House, near Frome ©E.L.Dineley
Image by kind permission of Peter Fitzgerald [6]

Berkley House became Abigail Prowse's home until her death in 1763 at the age of 79. She has been described as '*one of the most accomplished women of her time, admired for her excellent understanding, extensive knowledge and agreeable manners*'[7] It is good to know that she would have had the pleasure of living in her new house for a further thirty years. There can be little doubt that in the last few years of her life, as she walked through the hall at Berkley, she would have looked many times at the portrait of her only son. It would have been painted soon after she decided to redecorate the hall in a more baroque style.[8] Consequently, the Rococo frame would have been chosen to suit the setting in which it would be displayed. The inclusion of the circular building plan in place of the book of Parliamentary Bills and the addition of the architect's dividers may simply have reflected a fond mother's wish to be reminded of a more creative and personal aspect of her son's talents and interests, rather than his role and fine reputation as a Parliamentarian.

Between 1740 and 1767, Thomas Prowse was returned unopposed five times as MP for one of the Somerset seats and acted as the Recorder of Axbridge for many years.[9] It would therefore seem appropriate that a portrait on display in his home at Compton Bishop would highlight his duty to ensure that the local burgesses kept within the law. The fact that this painting was probably donated to the Town Trust in its original carved and gilded frame, typical of the seventeenth century, substantiates the theory that it had previously been at Compton House, built in the 1600s.[10]

Thus, it was not difficult to discover a logical explanation for the existence of two almost identical portraits of Thomas Prowse, one acknowledging his achievements as an amateur architect, the other recognising his reputation as a highly respected and long-standing local Member of Parliament. What has proved much harder to understand is evidence that, by 1941, there also existed a third three-quarter length portrait of Thomas Prowse very similar to the one at Berkley House. This, in fact, was an intentional copy and was, without doubt, painted in about 1940 by Bath artist, Reginald Wright, long-serving City Librarian and then curator of the Victoria Art Gallery. Mistaking the circular drawing to be a plan of the Circus in Bath, Wright became convinced that the man in the portrait had to be the City's famous architect, John Wood the Elder.

A black and white photograph of Wright's copied version of the Berkley portrait is now at Bath Record Office. A label on the back confirms that it had been photographed by G. Bolwell in 1941 and had then been among the collection at the Victoria Art Gallery.[11] It is difficult to imagine that it could have completely disappeared, yet numerous enquiries and diligent searches have so far failed to discover the present whereabouts of Reginald Wright's copy, or confirm that it still exists. Wright died in 1963, aged 74, by which time his firmly held belief that the gentleman in the portrait was John Wood the Elder had become generally acknowledged – and not only in Bath. Until recently, an entry for Berkley House, near Frome, a Grade II listed building, could be found on the Historic England website.[12]

Compton House Today

A description of the interior of the house (not seen) particularly referred to '... *a portrait believed to be of John Wood of Bath, carved rococo decoration to frames of c1750.*' A framed or unframed print of Wright's copy can still be bought online. Not exactly incorrectly, yet perhaps misleadingly, it is described as follows:

Thought to be John Wood the Elder, although there are several different versions of this painting. Copy of a portrait at Berkley House, near Frome. Versions of this painting exist without what appears to be a plan of the Circus [13]

Surprisingly, evidence has even been found in correspondence among Evelyn Newby's research papers at the Paul Mellon Centre for Studies in British Art confirming that until Giles Worsley's article was published in *Country Life in* 1988 – and presumably for many years before that – this same portrait had been wrongly indexed in the records at the National Portrait Gallery in London as *John Wood the Elder, attributed to William Hoare.* [14]

Intriguing questions are bound to be raised regarding the third painting: how had the portrait at Berkley House been brought to the attention of Reginald Wright in the first place and why had he been so overwhelmingly convinced that it had to be a portrait of John Wood that he decided to paint a copy of it? It seems very likely that a brief paragraph and photograph of the Berkley portrait – which appeared in 1939 in the Journal of the Royal Institution of British Architects under the heading *Wood of Bath?* [15] – might well provide the answer.

The heading was clearly designed to arouse interest, but sadly destined to be very misleading. Mr John Hatton, director of the Bath Pump Room, was the man who hoped to discover more about this 'mystery' portrait, although how the image might have come into his possession was not revealed. He had already consulted most of the recognised authorities, including Bath historian Mowbray Green and the National Portrait Gallery, but was hoping '... *that some architect might know of a portrait of either John Wood the Elder or his son in private possession, information about which ...... may help in the identification of this picture.*'

It seems unlikely that anyone came forward at the time, either to dismiss the speculative idea that the portrait might depict one of the Woods of Bath or to confirm the real identity of the gentleman in the painting. In a city long deprived of any portraits of its two most renowned architects, this meant that it became all too tempting for people to jump to the wrong conclusion. Who else, other than John Wood senior, or possibly his son, would have been portrayed holding an architect's dividers in his right hand, with a plan closely resembling the Circus clearly visible on the table in front of him?

One mystery still remained concerning the original Berkley version of the portrait. The fact that Prowse had been *'a country gentleman with a practical interest in architecture'* [16] would explain the inclusion of the dividers, but, unless some evidence could be found to link him with a building project requiring a circular plan, it was difficult to attach any particular significance to the architectural drawing in the portrait, which, understandably, might easily be mistaken for John Wood the Elder's design for the Circus.

Worsley's claim that Thomas Prowse had been an eminent amateur architect was well justified. With Sanderson Miller, Prowse contributed to designs for Hagley Hall, Worcestershire and the Shire Hall in Warwick. He designed Wicken Church in Northamptonshire, as well as Wicken House, inherited when he married Elizabeth Sharp in 1731. He also drew up plans for Hatch

Court, Somerset and alterations to Kimberley Hall in Norfolk.[17] The rectangular Temple of Harmony at Halswell Park, Somerset, designed for his friend Sir Charles Kemeys-Tynte, was completed in 1767, the year of Prowse's death.[18] None of these buildings appear to include any obvious exterior feature that might have required a circular drawing.

One of Prowse's earliest projects, however, was the re-designing of Copt Hall in Essex, which he worked on with Sir Roger Newdigate and John Sanderson in the early 1740s. These early plans were never adopted, but they did include a drawing of an enclosed central Rotunda. Although this did not closely resemble the plan depicted in the Berkley portrait, it was at least circular.[19]

It may have been the planned Rotunda for Copt Hall that inspired the interior octagonal dome in St Mary's Church in Berkley, rebuilt in 1751 and now thought to have been designed by Thomas Prowse.[20] It is interesting that the delicate patterns of filigree stucco work used to embellish the dome reflect the Rococo-style decor introduced at Berkley House in the 1750s by Abigail Prowse.

Early Plan for Interior Rotunda for Copt Hall, Essex. RIBA Collection

Interior Dome of Berkley Church. By kind permission of Philip Bendall [21]

These designs may not entirely account for the circular plan in the portrait, but they would without doubt have held some personal significance for Thomas Prowse's mother, Abigail. It would be interesting to know what Thomas Prowse might have thought had he known that one day his portrait would be mistaken for a painting of John Wood, the renowned Bath architect. Prowse was clearly a likeable, charitable, much admired and greatly respected gentleman. As a lesser known amateur architect, he could well have found the idea pleasing and mildly amusing. He was buried at St John's Church, Axbridge, not far from his house in Compton Bishop. His elaborate memorial inscription reads:

... He discharged his duty in Parliament with ability, integrity and honour .... ever attentive rather to promote the Interest and Happiness of others than his own ...

It says much for the quality of the portraits of Thomas Prowse that they not only portrayed what he looked like, but captured exactly the estimable man he was.

'... Few have lived so greatly beloved or died so universally lamented.'

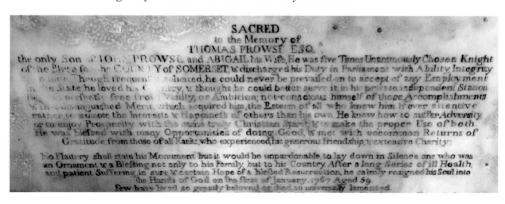

Memorial to Thomas Prowse Esq. St John's Church, Axbridge, Somerset

References:

[1] Giles Worsley: Berkley House, Somerset: *Country Life Magazine*, 19th May 1988, pp.168-171

[2] Photograph of Portrait of Thomas Prowse: Portraits Po-S, Box 11, Evelyn Newby Archive GB3010; The Paul Mellon Centre for Studies in British Art, London UK

[3] Information from John Page, Trustee of Axbridge Town Trust

[4] Michael McGarvie, F.S.A. *St Mary's Berkley, A History and Guide*, p.16

[5] See ref. 1, p.170

[6] Photograph of Berkley House from: Peter Fitzgerald: *Nathaniel Ireson of Wincanton: Architect, Master Builder & Potter*; published by Dovecote Press, 2016

[7] Memorial Inscription to Abigail Prowse in the church of St John The Baptist, Axbridge; quoted in St Mary's, Berkley, A History and Guide, p.18

[8] See ref.1, p. 171

[9] www.axbridgetownhall.co.uk/history/artefacts/

[10] See ref. 3

[11] Bath Record Office: Local Studies Photograph Collections: Portraits/Wood, John the Elder

[12] www.historicengland.org.uk/listing/the-list/ : Berkley House: List entry: 1058192. [Information quoted here accessed 07/06/2021 – now revised]

[13] www.bathintime.co.uk: Image Reference: 48838; accessed 05/11/22

[14] Portraits Po-S, Box 11, Evelyn Newby Archive GB3010 The Paul Mellon Centre London UK: Correspondence between Evelyn Newby and the curator of 18th Century Portraits at the National Portrait Gallery; July 1988

[15] Royal Institution of British Architects Journal, Vol. 46, No. 11 (1939), 536

[16] Quoted (1995) by Lewis Namier & John Brooke in The House of Commons,1754-1790, Vol. 1, p 336: referenced H. Colvin: *A Biographical Dictionary of British Architects 1600-1840*, p.479

[17] Howard Colvin: *A Biographical Dictionary of British Architects 1600-1840*: John Murray, London, 1978; Thomas Prowse: pp.666-667

[18] The Temple of Harmony: designed by Thomas Prowse: https://halswellpark.wordpress.com/2016/01/22/the-temple-of-harmony/, accessed 05/11/22

[19] RIBA pix Ref. No.: RIBA20081: Image date 1740: Architects/designer: Newdigate, Sir Roger (1719-1806), Prowse, Thomas (1708-1767), Sanderson, John (d. 1774)

[20] Michael McGarvie, F.S.A.: *St Mary's Berkley, A History and Guide*, p19

[21] Philip Bendall: Bath Burial Index: https://www.batharchives.co.uk/cemeteries/berkley

Edited version of an article by David Crellin and Penny Gay published in November 2021 on the website of the History of Bath Research Group

With particular thanks to local historians Alastair MacLeay (Frome), John Page and Margaret Jordan (Axbridge and Compton Martin) for their guidance and help. Their extensive knowledge of this area of Somerset and in-depth interest in the history of Thomas Prowse and his family have contributed so much to this research project.

FROME PORTRAITS 26

THOMAS THYNNE 2nd MARQUESS OF BATH 1765-1837.

Thomas Thynne after Thomas Lawrence

The 2nd Marquess was a benefactor of Frome, giving up land and buildings so that Bath Street, a new wide road could be created leading south from the town centre. He set aside land for allotments for a hundred families. "I have been told that at a certain hour in the morning he would admit the humblest persons in his parish, listen to their little concerns, and advise them. He was one of the few who well understood for what purposes rank, wealth, and influence, are conferred."(Thomas Bunn). It was he that commissioned the Jeremiah Cruse map of Frome in 1813.

NAISH'S STREET IN THE CENSUS

Sue Leather

(Based on the short Zoom talk given to the Frome Society in May 2021)

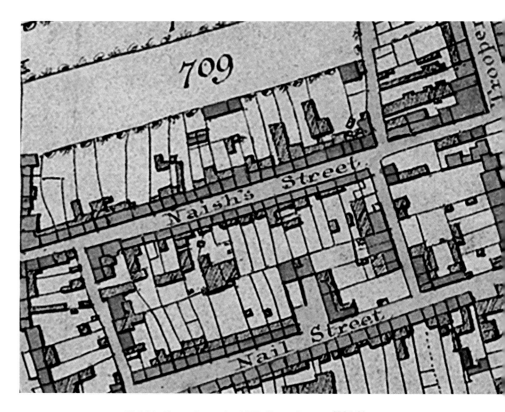

Naish's Street from the 1813 Cruse Survey (FSLS)

In the nineteenth century censuses, (taken from 1841) it can be a bit of a headache working out who lived where as numbering of the houses was usually fairly random or non-existent. There were no hard and fast rules until quite late into the century and many census enumerators had their own systems of numbering. There are currently only 47 houses in Naish's Street, even though the numbering of those houses goes up to 64, as it does in the censuses. Over the years, houses have been divided up or amalgamated while several now bricked-up front doors are still visible. There were also houses in what are now the car parks in Baker Street and Trinity Row, accessed by alleyways off Naish's Street.

At the bottom end of the street - now Wiltshire's Barton - was Ford's Lane and Moon's Yard. From 1881, both were included as part of Naish's Street using numbers 31 to 37, so those numbers no longer exist. These houses were among the poorest in the area - this entry is from 1871:

2 [houses] Uninhabited one of them being in ruins & converted into a Saw pit.

Given that there were generally around 60 houses in the street, the population density was quite high. From 1841, there were about 300 residents (an average of about five per house), but by the 1890s that number had started to dwindle and, by 1939, there were only 200 residents (averaging about 3.5 per house).

Throughout the nineteenth century, only about a quarter of those living in Naish's Street had **not** been born in Frome; there was a smattering of Londoners, but most of the others came from outlying villages (Beckington, Mells, Nunney, Rode and Leigh-on-Mendip) and from over the border in Wiltshire. The vast majority of those living in the street - between 70-80% - were born in Frome, many spending their entire lives in the Trinity area.

As the years went on, a few residents stated that they had been born in Wales. There was migration from Frome to the South Wales coalfields in some numbers during the nineteenth century, and a few families returned to Frome with children having been born in Wales in the interim. The largest age group throughout the century were those aged between 11 and 20, with many of the younger ones already working.

+ Benjamin Hopkins	Head	Mar	46		Carpenter	
Elizabeth	do	Wife	Mar		40	
John	do	Son		14		Errand Boy
Elizabeth	do	Daur		12		Factory Girl Wool

		Name	Age (M)	Age (F)	Occupation	Born in county
	1	Thomas ? Davey	30		Coach Driver	Yes
		Henry Hutson	45		Ag Lab	Yes
		Mary do		30		No
		Elizabeth do		15	Shoe Hoskey	Yes
		Harriet do		15	do	Yes
		Lucis a do		15	do	Yes
		Ann do		13	do	Yes
		William do	4 mo			Yes
	1	Samuel Button	45		Weaver	Yes
		Ann do		45	do	Yes
		William do	20		Ag Lab	Yes
		Samuel do	21		Woollen Worker	Yes
	1	Betty Yeomst		75	Pauper	Yes
	1	John Dredge	20		Ag Lab	Yes
		Elizabeth do		20	Taylor	Yes
		Alfred do	3			Yes
		Emma a do		7 mo		Yes
		Richard Cuzner	40		Weaver	Yes
	1	Richard Bunn	75		Maltster	No
		Sarah do		15		Yes
		John Pickford	75		Carpenter	Yes
		James Hillier	70		Weaver	No

Around a third of the population was aged 10 and under, but, by 1911, that proportion had dwindled to only one-sixth of the residents. At the other end of the scale, there were always one or two people over 80, a very advanced age.

The phrase 'All human life is here' could have been invented for Naish's Street - there has always been a mix of social classes within the street and, even now, there is a mixture of social housing and privately-owned and -rented properties. Along with that came a wide range of occupations - the 1841 census shows coach driver, agricultural labourer, wire worker, weaver, woollen worker, pauper, tailor, maltster and carpenter on this page alone.

Some professionals and those with larger incomes did live in the street - teachers, a land agent, Inland Revenue staff, a solicitor, an insurance agent and those with independent means. During that century, more people began to 'go out' to work, rather than work from home. A common sight throughout the nineteenth century was Chelsea and Greenwich pensioners, those discharged from the Army and Navy through injury or illness and many of these managed to find work to supplement their pensions.

Jacob Hurd, a weaver, had joined the Somerset Regiment as a 16-year-old in 1793 and had risen to the rank of Serjeant by 1795. He received a campaign medal with clasp at the Siege of Alexandria in Egypt in 1801, having also served in the West Indies and Holland. Jacob contracted an eye disease in December 1808 which left him blind in both eyes and he was given a pension the following year. It appears that, despite his blindness, he was able to return to his trade as a weaver.

Joseph Wimpey served in the Peninsular War, the Medal Roll stating that he received three clasps (at Corunna, Ciudad Rodrigo and Badajoz). He was discharged unfit in 1815, having lost an eye and suffering from rheumatism. He returned to Frome and married; he and his wife were in Naish's Street in 1851, but by 1861 Joseph had become the toll bar keeper at Bunns Lane near Gare Hill.

Most women were employed within the home; many of those in paid employment were servants and laundresses, dressmakers and milliners. But in 1871 - noted by a possibly scandalised enumerator - three young women 'keep a brothel'.

The woollen industry accounted for much of female paid employment, but this industry decreased during the nineteenth century as local mills failed to keep pace with change. Many men were also employed in the woollen industry meaning that, in 1841, 81 residents of Naish's Street were employed in textiles; this was reduced by 50% by 1871 and, by 1901, there were only 15 workers, most of whom were at the silk mill.

In 1841, a number of men were employed as wire drawers. The Cabble family was one that became employed almost exclusively in wire manufacture. Edward Cabble, died aged 49 in 1844 and this seems to have been the catalyst for the remainder of his family to emigrate to America. The eldest son, already married in 1841 and living on The Butts, founded a wire manufacture firm in New York with two of his brothers; other siblings and his widowed mother followed.

ELIJAH CABBLE.

The last surviving brother, Elijah Cabble, died in 1903 in Brooklyn aged 71. His obituary, published in a trade journal, mentions that he was born in Frome and came to America aged 15.

"Being possessed by inheritance of a rugged constitution and an indomitable will, and the fine moral stuff of which the captains of industry are made, his business rise was rapid and substantial. "Mr Cabble was one of the founders of the Dime Savings Bank of Williamsburg and was a director in the institution.

The funeral services were held on Tuesday evening of this week. The Cabble home was unable to hold the great number of friends, relatives, business associates and employees who assembled to pay their last respects."

From 1861, there was an increase in men working in foundries with the continuing development of heavy industry in the town, and there was always a fair number of labourers in a variety of trades and industries among Naish's Street residents. From 1851, those labouring on the land decreased dramatically and in 1891 and 1901 there were none at all who lived in the street, despite being so close to the edge of town.

Another major employer was, of course, Butler & Tanner, at their print works in Selwood Road. In 1871, only three residents were working in the printing industry; this had increased to 14 by 1881 and had doubled 10 years later, undoubtedly due to the proximity of the street to the Selwood Works. From the 1870s, men at Butler & Tanner worked a 54.5 hour week, from 6.30am to 6pm Monday to Friday with breaks for breakfast and lunch, as well as working until 1 o'clock on Saturdays; women and girls worked slightly fewer hours, as did the proof readers.

The Printing Works. Selwood

Conversely, probably because of the distance to Frome Station, not many were employed on the railways, the main exception being in 1851 when the line onward from Frome was actually being built. **Joseph Kerslake** seems to have been a railway navvy throughout the 1840s, judging by the places of birth of his children: Bridgwater station opened in 1841, Tiverton in 1848 and Frome in 1850. It was estimated at the time that more than 300 navvies lived in Frome in 1851, along with their wives and children.

Adam Clarke	Lodger	u	14		
Joseph Kerslake	Head	Mar 45		Rail Lab	Devon Sanford Pevil
Mary do	Wife	Mar			Devon Topsham
Thomas do	Son	u	15	Rail Lab	do do
John do	Son	14			Somerset Bridgwater
Mary do	Daur		4	Scholar	Devon Tiverton
William do	Son		2	do	do Topsham
Priscilla do	Daur				Somerset Frome
William Byrne	Lodger	25		Rail Lab	do do
William Hodge	Head	May 24		Rail Lab	Devon Exeter
Sarah do	Wife	Mar			do Topsham

Another family, living in Naish's Street in 1841, had connections to the railways. Their eldest son, **John Tarrent**, became a railway excavator and, in 1871, was living in Yorkshire where he was working on the construction of the Settle to Carlisle line. More than 6000 men were employed there between 1869 and 1876 and many hundreds were killed in accidents and outbreaks of smallpox during that time. It's tempting to think that a Naish's Street boy may well have worked on the construction of the famous Ribblehead Viaduct completed in 1874. By 1886, John had returned to Frome and married, and he stayed here until his death in 1925.

Until well into the twentieth century, there were shops in Naish's Street, among the last being the Britannia Stores on the corner of Naish's Street and Vallis Way. Number 6 was a bakery for many years before being taken over by the Paniccia family as their ice cream parlour - in this photo, one of Paniccia's vans can be seen outside number 6. Number 20 was also a bakery, run by the same family for more than 50 years, and, at other times, there have been other provision shops along the street.

Further down the social scale were those in very low paid jobs, such as rag sorting and bill posting. There were always a number of paupers and those receiving parish relief. Some were assisted by Emma Sheppard, the well-known local philanthropist, among them in Naish's Street being Samuel and Ann Button, whom she referred to as 'The Old Buttons'. About half of the families living in Naish's Street were non-conformists, possibly because of the presence of a Baptist chapel in the street (now Paniccia Court flats). Some residents are known to have been baptised or registered at Rook Lane Chapel on Bath Street, Zion Chapel on Whittox Lane and Badcox Chapel on Catherine Street; many are buried in the Dissenters' Cemetery in Vallis Road. Additional information was occasionally given by the enumerator. In 1861, the added the comment **the husband is in a lunatic asylum** against Elizabeth Pope's name.

Her shoemaker husband, Edward, can be found at the County Asylum in Wells as 'EW a pauper lunatic' - it was customary to refer to those in mental health institutions or in prison by their initials only. By 1871, Edward had returned to his family and they remained in Naish's Street until his death, but he never went back to shoemaking and earned a living outdoors thereafter, firstly as an agricultural labourer and then as a gardener. Edward and Elizabeth both died in the early 1890s and are buried in Vallis Road Dissenters' Cemetery.

Not only does the census provide a snapshot of the street every ten years, but it also provides a springboard for further discoveries from other sources to 'flesh out the bones'.

There is a comment against Emma Wheeler's entry in 1861: **the husband is in prison.**
Sure enough, the census for HMP Shepton Mallet reveals one HW (ie Henry Wheeler), a tailor from Frome. Criminal records show that he had a history of assaulting his wife and, on this occasion, he was serving two months' imprisonment. On his release, he seems to have returned to his family, since another child was born in 1863. However, Henry absconded soon afterwards and spent the remainder of his life in South Wales, where he appears to have married bigamously and had a second family. Emma was left to fend for herself and her children. She worked as a general servant and as a charwoman before entering the Frome Union Workhouse, where she died in 1892.

This 1871 entry is for Elizabeth J Moore who stated, **husband in America.**
By using US immigration records and American censuses, it is known that her husband, Farnham Moore, first went to America in 1852 with his father, and he was recorded on the 1860 US census in Michigan. He married in America, but his wife died soon afterwards and

Farnham returned to Frome. In March 1865, he married Elizabeth Jane Gunning Harvey at St John's church and they had two children. Farnham left again for America just before this census was taken in 1871, possibly not knowing that Elizabeth was pregnant with their third child. He had come back to Naish's Street by the end of 1874 and he remained in Frome until his death in 1911.

Albert Gane was a five-year-old boy in 1871. He joined the Royal Navy on his eighteenth birthday and appears on the 1881 census in Devonport on HMS *Impregnable*, a training ship. His Naval record shows that he qualified as a signaller and, by 1888, had become a leading signaller, despite having spent a period in Kilmainham Gaol in Ireland. However, by March 1890, he had deserted and was not apprehended for 20 months, when he was sentenced to 87 days in Bodmin Gaol. Even then, he remained in the navy until, in October 1892, he jumped ship in Argentina. There is nothing more heard of him in naval records, but he suddenly re-appears in London in 1930 when he married, following which he lived in Hammersmith. By the outbreak of the Second World War, he and his wife had moved to Earls Court and he was employed as a motor driver. He died in July 1946 aged 81 and is buried in a common grave in Brompton Cemetery.

And finally, Lydia Pope's husband was **in Ireland** in 1871. Cicero Sydney Pope left for Ireland between 1868 and 1871, and was buried there a few days before Christmas 1874 aged 41. The

POPE Cicero Sydney.

Effects under £200.

Resworn June 1876 under £450.

3 February.   Administration of the effects of Cicero Sydney Pope late of Frome in the County of **Somerset** Cooper who died 22 December 1874 at 140 James-street in the City of Dublin in Ireland was granted at **Wells** to Lydia Pope of Frome Widow the Relict.

probate index gives the place of death, date, the value of his estate and names his widow, Lydia, as executor. Lydia brought her husband's body back home to Frome and he is buried in Holy Trinity churchyard, as the church register records.

The street in 1886 from the Ordnance Survey. (FSLS)

Credits: The National Archives, Principal Probate Registry, Holy Trinity Church, Find My Past, Ancestry and the Frome Society for Local Study.

ANCIENT CHEESE RITUAL

Cheap Street 1934

This picture is dated September 1934 and is alleged to show a 'dairymaid' placing a cheese in the leat that runs down Cheap Street in an ancient custom to bring good luck to the annual Cheese Show. However, contributors to the *Bath Chronicle* had their doubts, and one letter dated November 1933 referred to a similar photo the year before consisting of, 'two women christening the cheese in readiness for the Frome Cheese Show'. It was described as an ancient custom', continues the correspondent, 'has this occurrence any historical foundation and how far back can it be traced'?

A reply was printed the following week, 'I have been assured by friends living at Frome that the photograph in question was 'posed' and although a similar effort was made about three years ago to institute this as an 'ancient custom' it has no history behind it.'

That, of course, was almost ninety years ago and so it has some history behind it now; ancient customs have to start somewhere so isn't it about time that this worthy superstition was revived?

PATRICK MONTAGUE BROWNE

& THE DISCOVERY OF BROWNES' HOLE*

Andrew Edwards & Colin Wisby

This article is taken from the first part of a detailed report entitled *'Brownes' Hole, Stoke St Michael, Frome, Somerset.* and provides a background to the family and the initial investigation of the cave. Part two concerning the finds and further information will appear in future issue. *Ed*

Brownes' Hole main entrance in 2022 (Andrew Edwards)

Born in Frome, in the Autumn of 1930, Patrick was the only son of Mary and Leslie Browne a coal merchant, with offices at 27 Christchurch Street East, Frome and the nearby Wallbridge railway sidings. Patrick is thought to have been the only grandson of Rhodesian pioneer Henry Browne[1] who was born in 1870 in Brentford, Middlesex and who married Laura Bendle in 1896 in Devon. Henry Browne travelled to the north of Rhodesia as either a farmer or a copper mine prospector and although his precise reasons for being there are not established, it would be nice to think that Patrick gained his interest in mining together with his grandfather's love of exploring from his ancestor. Grandmother Laura was born in Frome in 1871 to Frederick Bendle, born in1842, the founder of the coal merchants which was to become F. Bendle and Son. In the 1881 census they were living at 28 Christchurch Street, Frome but by 1891 Frederick Bendle was widowed.

Frederick and Laura Bendle had a son, William, born in 1879 who married Dorothy Helen Lyon on 15 August 1910 who at the age of 32 became a Doctor of Medicine. This left the Bendle coal merchants of Frome without an heir until Leslie Browne Patrick's father was born in Sidbury, Devon in 1901. On 28 October 1929, the registration of marriage between Leslie M Browne and Mary T Reynolds (Patrick's mother) is listed as 'St Thomas', Exeter. By the 1911 census Harry Browne was living at Tents Hill House, Mells, finding work as a rock excavator in the local quarries. Leslie, worked for Frederick Bendle at the family coal merchants and Patrick Browne and attended the preparatory school for Frome Grammar followed by the prestigious King's School, Bruton. Weekends were spent exploring Mendip's caves and swallets with his father Leslie.

Patrick Montague Browne.

Occasional holidays were taken in Scotland and North Wales, one specific location being the Old Barn at Blaen Nant Farm, in the Ogwen Valley not far from Tryfan. The cost varied according to whether they stayed at the dry end of the hut which was 6d per night or the wet end which was 3d.

Patrick's first job was about a year in the offices of the family firm Bendle, Coal Merchants of Frome. The Great Western Railway provided sidings at a place called Bendle's Wharf now housing but retaining the name to this day. The original mineral railway still exists and is used by the Whatley Limestone Quarry of Mells, owned and operated by Hanson Aggregates. Quarrying industries still provide a significant source of employment for the people of Frome.

5, Trinity Parade, Frome. Home to the Browne family.

Patrick graduated from King's School, Bruton and studied mine engineering at Manchester University. For part of his time there he lived in Bethesda and pursued his love of climbing and mountaineering as well as working for a mining company in North Wales. The temptation to go climbing with his friends whilst on vacation from the university was always in his mind. He was described later as absolutely fearless in his caving and climbing activities. Manchester was 106 miles from the Ogwen Valley but there was an adequate rail service owing to the quarrying activities at Bethesda. On one occasion, at the age of 21, Patrick led a group consisting of himself and two friends to a base camp in the next valley from Ogwen, at the Llanberis Pass which he had visited twice before.

At the foothills of Mount Snowdon, the highest mountain in England and Wales, they pitched a simple tent close to some crags - Clogwyn y Grochan which they planned to climb. His associates were Derek Greenwood a 16-year-old schoolboy from London and Bryan Helsby, from Gorton, Manchester, an apprentice machinist. On Monday 20 August 1951 they began the assent.

After the first pitch, both Greenwood and Helsby tied themselves to an appropriate rock. Browne was progressing towards the second pitch. His ascent progressed well, until he reached an overhang, just before reaching the top he lost his foothold and was heard to say "I can't make it !I'm coming off !" and Patrick fell 60 feet past his companions. His second prepared himself, took hold of the rope and took in the slack.

Briefly, the rope was taut, but, being made from damp hemp material, it was not able to take his weight and the second found himself holding onto a loose length of rope.

Browne firstly crashed into the rock and the rope had broken at a running belay, he fell headlong into the rocks at the bottom and died instantly from fractures to his cranium.

He was laid to rest in Caernarfon, Gwynedd, North Wales. Patrick was just 20 and despite his young years was said to have made a great contribution to the exploration of underground Mendip and the Bristol Exploration Club to which he had belonged for many years.

Patrick ascending Mount Tryfan on the North Buttress route on the Eastern face.

The Discovery of Brownes' Hole

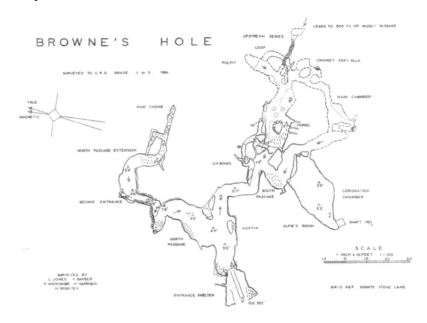

Survey of Brownes' Hole Cave. (Frome Museum)

The first published reference to Brownes' Hole appears on page 122 of Herbert E. Balch's famous book, *Mendip, Its Swallet Caves and Rock Shelters*. Patrick Browne, a pupil of King's School, Bruton whilst visiting Stoke Lane Swallet, explored what can be described as a burrow entrance hole that was wide enough for a fox or badger to enter. The discovery is estimated to have been made by Patrick in August 1947. What emerged after further exploration was a dry swallet that we now call 'Brownes' Hole' named after him.

The entrance is horizontal and faces approximately south west which would have offered a warm aspect in the afternoon sunshine for its inhabitants. It is not known for how long the cave has been dry but the possibility of either seismic activity from the nearby Moon's Hill Volcano or quarrying activity could have diverted the water course that originally helped to carve out the interior passages. It is worth mentioning that the quarry owners, Messrs Cullen and Treasure, were concerned that they did not harm the cave by halting further works close by.

Patrick Browne's synopsis of Brownes' Hole Cave:

A sub-water table, phreatic with definite current flow to the West. The bedding joint plane anastomosis seen in various points. Water table leaving the Cave clear of mud fill and dry. There was no clay fill epoch and the Calcite formations were formed. Vadose action soon ensued but this was in no wise severe. It took the form of a meandering stream of small size, laying red grit in the terminal tunnel, forming the sink pot by vadose abrasive and solutional action. Also, welling up the stream mineralised and began to meander up the entrance tunnel into the Valley. This valley probably integrated with the cave in phreatic times forming a great, clear rising of subwater table flow

For some reason the Vadose stream ceased to flow three or four times for considerable periods of time until there came either a second rising of the water table or the great floods. At any rate the Vadose stream's work at modification was ended by the partial filling of the Cave by turbulent muddy waters, with no great current, welling up from the depths of the system. Although this can hardly be considered a phreatic state of affairs, the Cave- making continued by solution as if it were. Air was trapped in pockets in "the forge". This surface was below the true surface of the water. It was a "depressed surface". Gradually the Cave was filled with mud, clay and silt from the slowly moving waters. Another change deposited stratified layers of sand. All passages below the water were soon filled with mud. Again, the water table fell. The top of the fill was lowered by compaction and Vadose conditions reclaimed the Cave and are now in the process of removing the fill.

Patrick Browne , Wednesday 4th May 1949

The other members of the party responsible for the initial digging were; Leslie Browne (father), Mrs Browne (mother), Messrs Kendrick of Frome, Mr Stock (the farmer) and many volunteers, who opened up the first 80 feet of the cave and caverns in the first three months of the operation.[2] This number of people working in a relatively dry cave environment in the summer made remarkably good progress. Descriptions of the interior of Brownes' Hole include the entrance passageways and the entrance itself is situated on a relatively steep bank currently surrounded by deciduous woodland and heart's tongue ferns. In order to gain entry one has to huddle down slightly to approximately 5 feet in height and to continue in this manner for some 20 feet after which you arrive at a left bend with a narrow tunnel. This is 10 feet in length which has to be negotiated on the stomach and work along on the elbows.

After this short crawl it is possible to walk along a crevice in an upright position. Finally, there is a 10-foot-high bank mud and silt and a rope is advised at this point. After this you have to negotiate around a rock face and travel through a narrow opening into a chamber where there are many stalagmites and stalactites. Most of these chambers were described as having been silted up and much of the work had to be carried out on hands and knees or flat on the stomach in order to avoid the stalactites. Finally, one arrives at a room in which it is possible to stand and it is believed that this is the location of the original watercourse - possibly the source of much of the silt that had been discovered. At this point there is a sheer rise to the roof. To one side is a remarkable formation called 'The Pulpit' and facing this formation is another resembling a waterfall. [3]

The Excavations

From the description of the main passages it is clear that the first 80 feet are relatively simple to negotiate. This process was accompanied by the careful emptying of the silt onto sorting tables which were erected further up the valley of Stoke Lane in the sunlight. In 1947 at least four named individuals were constantly involved. It is assumed that they created a chain gang within the cave by means of buckets passed to the long passage at the entrance. Surnames that signed the log regularly were; Lucy, Browne, Course, Stock, Lambert, McGuire, Kendrick, Chivers, Percy and Candy. It seems that there were no significant incidents or accidents reported in the late 1940s probably due to a consistent, experienced and trained team of workers. Personal protective equipment included safety helmets and lamps to ensure that the collection of artefacts was more meticulous.

The 'sorting table' at Brownes' Hole (Paul Stillman)

Reading the early diaries from 1947, the main area for finding faunal remains seems to have been the cave entrance. Bones were taken to Herbert Balch, a self- taught naturalist from Wells for cleaning and more specific identification. Balch had considerable experience of identifying faunal material from caves and was regarded as a specialist. The following reports are taken from the dig diaries.

Leslie Browne was responsible for the removal of mud and silt from the entrance area prior to 4 August 1947. There is a report of many bones being found on 12 August 1947 in the wide chamber, presumably after the ten feet crawl and just before the muddy vertical climb. The bones here were mainly badger and, in the stalactite, chamber more bones of badger and fox were found. At this juncture the Brownes' concluded that the stalactites were formed many years ago when considerably more water was entering the cave.

The final passage was opened by Patrick on 31 August 1947, where he again found bones of badger and fox. It was sensed that a steep exit route was leading out of the caves as air movement was felt. The slow and meticulous digging at the primary entrance revealed pieces of pottery and flint indicating human habitation. At the entrance the bones of a small horse were also found together with a red deer antler.

On 5 October 1947 a table was set up outside the cave for sorting the bones that were recovered from the main entrance passage. Horse teeth were found close to the stalactite formation and the team appear to have taken great care focussing on specific parts of the cave to explore on each occasion sorting the silt from each section before moving onto the next with meticulous attention.

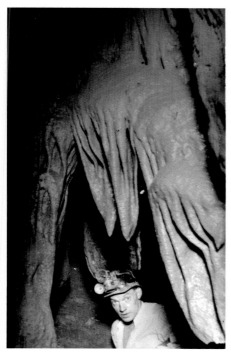

There are references to clearing out various chambers such as on 13 October when they were collecting the smallest artefacts of bone material and within two months the operation went from one of excavation, observation, qualitative assessment onto quantitative summation of the finds. This evolution of approach was possibly due to the finding of bones at the entrance and with the involvement of Herbert Balch to be covered in part two of the report covering Dr Jackson's arrival to assist with the initial cataloguing of the finds.

On 19 October 1947 there is reference to a location called 'Stocks Point', a chamber from which a great deal of material was excavated. It took a whole day to painstakingly clean the excavated finds which consisted of charred material, bone and red deer antler. On 25 October 1947 along a passage leading from Stock's Chamber, a large canine tooth of what they believed to be a cave bear was recovered together with a large flint scraper.

The Curtain Chamber (Frome Museum)

On Saturday 28 August 1948, landowners, the Gilson Brothers, kindly lent the Brownes' a railway system or more specifically the rails. These were run into the cave with what appeared to be two carriages being used to move the silt and mud. It seems that this might have developed Patrick's interest in mining engineering, which he was to study at Manchester. This increased efficiency of moving heavy mud and silt reduced fatigue in the finders and enabled them to devote more time and energy to retrieving the important bone artefacts.

The diary has many references to excavations taking place in the Curtain Chamber where what is believed to be an adult human jaw bone was discovered as well as more red deer antler. In addition, a human tibia was found at that location, that had been flattened by squatting. Another human tibia was found at Stock's Point. One of these tibiae has been sent to the University of Bristol for radiocarbon dating. Additional finds from Stock's Point include hyena teeth.

Sunday 22 August 1948, in the section referred to as 'The Forge', Candy and the Browne family found two more canine teeth from hyena and many other bones, all meticulously cleaned and sorted. Explorations continued at another swallet local to Brownes' Hole in November 1948 in order to establish if any of the tunnels inter- connected as there was a wider concern about where water could enter should there be heavy rain.

Sunday 28 November 1948, excavations in the north passage recovered what are referred to as 'the usual', badger, chicken and rodent bones. By this time the term 'backdoor' or 'tradesmen's entrance' - a second opening had been established. It is interesting to note that a compass was used whilst surveying the cave underground and several references were made to this.

In 1949 Patrick was involved in explorations at 'Hunting Lodge Swallet', Priddy and the diary contains the only record of Patrick sustaining an injury when he slipped up with a bucket. The maximum number of bucket loads being hauled from Hunting Lodge seems to be nine in one shift.

Sunday 30 January 1949, a reference is made to diverting a stream that seems to flow from Stoke Lane Pond away from Brownes' Hole in order to secure safety inside the cave

Saturday 15 February 1949, a survey of Brownes' Hole was undertaken from the entrance to Tallenham Corner. This was undertaken by Patrick and Leslie Browne.

Sunday 20 March 1949, the backdoor entrance was further developed so that material could be hauled out through that exit by means of buckets and pulleys, they were assisted by Nash and Porter.

Saturday 26 March 1949 saw more meticulous sorting of silt taken from what they referred to as the deer tunnels.

Thursday 5 May 1949, Patrick mentions that he entered Brownes' Hole alone in order to conduct an archaeological survey. His task was to fix a baseline which he fixed from the 'Coffin' to the wall backing the 'St. C'. Patrick then writes his extensive survey and assessment of the cave, quoted at the start of this section.

Saturday 13 August 1949, the 1st Evercreech Scout Group camped in the field and one of the group members found either a hyena tooth and a deer tooth. An important juncture here is that the hyena tooth is described as *Hyaena Commis.* This may possibly have been identified by Balch with some knowledge of Pleistocene specimens as Dr Jackson had not yet arrived at Frome.

Sunday 25 September 1949, behind the Arch, part of hyena jaw with three teeth was recovered. Even at this stage significant finds were still being made.

Hyena jaw from the north passage approximately 57,000 BC (Frome Museum)

Saturday 24 February 1950, there are concerted efforts to continue surveying the north passage conducted by R. Kennedy and Leslie Browne. This work was described as unpleasant and slow but was completed in detail.

The Massive 'Bone Chamber' at Stoke Lane Slocker

[1] *Somerset Standard*, 24 August,1951
[2] *British Caver*, 1949, Volume 19 and reprinted from *Somerset Standard* 28 November 1947.
[3] *British Caver*, 1949 Volume 19
*The cave is known as Brownes' Hole (note the apostrophe) on the grounds that several members of the family were involved in the work. This is the spelling under which it is listed in the Mendip Cave Registry and other derived gazetteers. The Registrars are quite specific about details like this as they can be important in online literature searches.

SKULLS FOUND IN MENDIP CAVE ARE AROUND 4,000 YEARS OLD

In March the results of the radiocarbon dating of two skulls and a human tibia were released by the University of Bristol. This is a summary of their report.

Skulls from Mendip caves that have been held in a museum for over 80 years and whose age was unknown are from the Bronze Age scientists at the University of Bristol have found. Radiocarbon dating has shown that the two skulls are approximately 4,000 years old while a tibia dates back to just before the early Roman occupation of Britain. The bones were originally found during excavations of Brownes' Hole and Stoke Lane Slocker around the Mendip village of Stoke St Michael in the 1940s and housed in local museums, but have not been investigated since then.

Recently, interest rekindled in the collection at Frome Museum, and museum volunteers collaborated with the University of Bristol Speleological Society (UBSS) and the British Cave Research Association to determine their age. Andrew Chamberlain, Emeritus Professor of Bioarchaeology from the University of Manchester, who is studying the bone collections, said:

"The radiocarbon dating has shown that the bones found in the cave at Stoke Lane Slocker are the remains of people who lived during the Beaker period at the time of transition from the Neolithic to the Bronze Age. The Beaker period was a time of significant technological change, starting in about 2,400 BCE, when tools and weapons made from stone began to be replaced by artefacts made from copper and bronze.' The bones first came to the museum after excavations in Brownes' Hole and Stoke Lane Slocker, carried out in the 1940s by Pat Browne of Frome, Somerset. The bones from Brownes' Hole were found with an extensive collection of human and animal bones as well as artefacts, which have given archaeologists reason to believe that human use of this site dates back to the last Ice Age, and which offered some guideline as to the ages of the deposits.

However, the bones from Stoke Lane Slocker were far more enigmatic, found in a distant chamber alongside ash, charcoal, and red deer bones. A recent re-examination of the museum collection led volunteers to contact members of the UBSS, who joined the museum to secure a grant from the British Cave Research Association for radiocarbon dating of selected samples.

Human tibia from the late Iron Age (Mick Davis)

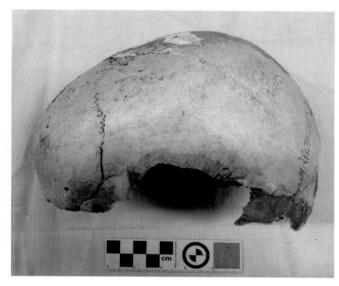

Two skulls from Stoke Lane Slocker and a tibia from Brownes' Hole were selected for testing by Professor Andrew Chamberlain and sent to Dr Timothy Knowles, Senior Research Associate at the Bristol Radiocarbon Accelerator Mass Spectrometry Facility (BRAMS) at the University of Bristol's School of Chemistry for assessment. The long bone from Brownes' Hole proved to date back to the last century BC, earlier than a Roman coin also found in the site.

Professor Chamberlain explained: "This is a period when a number of other caves in the Mendip region were used as natural burial chambers - the most well-known example being the cave at Wookey Hole. "The pottery and other artefacts found in the cave dated to a few hundred years later, after the Romans had invaded and overcome the native Iron Age communities."

The skulls proved to be much older - the radiocarbon dates showed that they were approximately 4,200 and 3,800 years old respectively about 400 years apart in date, raising interesting questions about the past use of the Stoke Lane Slocker site. The chamber in which the bones were found the Bone Chamber, is now only reachable by experienced cavers but would have been much easier to access at the time the skulls were deposited. Although there are plenty of Roman finds like those from Brownes' Hole, across the Mendip Hills, Bronze Age finds in caves are rarer though the earlier of the two is a very close contemporary of a human mandible recovered from a similarly deep location in Bone Hole, Cheddar Gorge and dated in 2008.

Professor Chamberlain said: "The radiocarbon dating shows that the cave was used as a burial place on two separate occasions during the Beaker period, separated in time by several hundred years. This may indicate that the cave was an important and memorable location that served as a long-standing place of burial and perhaps commemoration of the deceased by the Bronze Age people of this area." Graham Mullan, project leader at the UBSS, added: "The team hope that this additional information about Stoke Lane Slocker and Brownes' Hole will inspire future research into the prehistory and early history of the Mendip Hills."

SINGER'S CLOCK CASE 1880

From The Art Journal 1880

This design for a clock case of silver is by Mr. Herbert Singer, of Frome and the committee of the Goldsmiths' Company has awarded to it their first prize of £50. The artist has been educated in a good school, and has shown the value of early teaching. No doubt the eminent artist-manufacturer, 'Singer, of Frome,' has been indebted to the son, who has paid the debt he thus owes to the father. In Frome has been established an important art commerce, which enables it successfully to compete with the best ecclesiastical art work of the metropolis. The Church has been most beneficially supplied with art produce of the best order at comparatively small cost. Our engraving reminds us very forcibly of many of the bronze and silver clock cases, manufactured by the most important French houses, at the late Paris Exhibition.

Those who had an opportunity of viewing some of the beautiful productions in these two metals could not fail to perceive the results of the great attention bestowed by the French on this branch of industry. Within the last few years England, too, has been making vigorous efforts towards the goal of perfection, and the results are encouraging and successful. We are no longer afflicted with silver pug dogs, Skye terriers, bronze race-horses and jockeys in enamelled jackets, as specimens of British workmanship in silver and bronze. Mr. Singer's design is indicative of the improvement referred to. The subjects in the four panels at base. Spring, Summer, Autumn, and Winter, together with those above the dial. Morning, Noon, and Night, are to be executed in niello, the figures typical of Day and Night in silver repousse. The two groups on either side of these compartments represent Work and Play. It is a carefully studied design.

Walter Herbert Singer (1853-1922) was the son of John Webb Singer, and awarded a travelling scholarship from the Goldsmiths Company winning several prizes for his works: Paris 1878, London 1881 and Melbourne 1881.

§§§

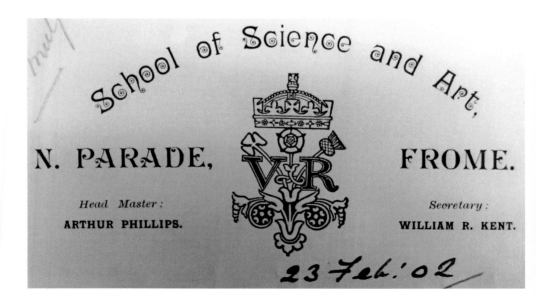

FROME MPs (PART 2: 1885-1950)

David Lassman

In Yearbook 25, the first part of this three-part series traced the Members of Parliament that represented Frome between 1832, when the Reform Act created a Parliamentary borough, until 1885, when it was dissolved. In this second part, the story continues from the creation of a new county division, until it too became obsolete in 1950.

In 1885, the Parliamentary borough of Frome, which had been created at the time of Great Reform Act of 1832, ceased to exist and the town became part of a new county division, the Frome Division of Somerset consisting of the entire north-eastern corner of the county, except for Bath (although several of its outlying villages and parishes were included, such as Weston, Batheaston and Swainswick).

With this change the constituency became a mixed one in terms of voters. There were those who resided in suburban areas, as well as agricultural villages. Added to this were the expanding mining communities in and around Radstock and the industrial centres of Twerton, which lay not far outside Bath centre and, by now, Frome itself, with the growth of companies such as Cockeys, Singers, and Butler & Tanner.

The result of this new demographic melting pot was that the Frome Division became a marginal constituency, fought over by the main parties of the day - Conservatives and Liberals – with the victor's majority rarely higher than a few hundred votes. As if to exemplify this, the 1885 election, which took place towards the end of that year, would see the successful candidate secure victory by 763 votes.

The 1885 general election was held between Tuesday 24 November and Friday 18 December 1885[1]and was contested between the Liberal, Lawrence James Baker (pictured above) and the Conservative Thomas Thynne. The 58-year-old Baker was a stockbroker and trustee of the London Stock Exchange, who was an expert in foreign bond dealings. However, it was also said that he was a generous benefactor who donated to charity and supported many initiatives, such as cutting taxes for the poor and free education. He had unsuccessfully stood as a candidate at least twice elsewhere, before being chosen for Frome at short notice in September, on the retirement through illness of Sir Henry Samuelson (the town's MP since 1876).

Baker's opponent was Thomas Thynne, whose family's estate was nearby Longleat (and who owned land and property in Frome). He was only 23 years old and would not graduate from

Balliol College, Oxford until the following year. He had been styled Viscount Weymouth since birth and before going up to university had been educated at Eton.

When the result of the 1885 election was announced, Baker had 4,735 votes to Thynne's 3,972 (maj. 763) in a turnout that numbered almost 83% of the electorate. His victory would be short-lived. Following the defeat of the 'Government of Ireland Bill'[2] the following year, another general election was called, and this took place throughout most of July 1886. By this time, Baker had somehow fallen out of favour and lost his selection for Frome. He was replaced by Godfrey Blundell Samuelson, the brother of earlier MP, Sir Henry Samuelson.

Thomas Thynne stood again but was now the older of the two candidates (by around eleven months). This time, the result went in his favour, and he enjoyed a 700 plus majority, securing 54.4% of the votes (4,348) against Samuelson's 45.6% (3,645). This calculated out as a +8.8 swing. He became the second Thynne to hold the seat, after his grandfather's brother, Edward, had represented the town between 1859-65. However, the loser – Samuelson – would also enter Parliament, the next year, when successful at a by-election in the Forest of Dean.

Thynne stood again in the 1892 election, but his opponent was the gentleman who would come to dominate the local political scene for the next quarter of a century. The 35-year-old Sir John Emmott Barlow (pictured below) was a British businessman and the latest Liberal candidate for Frome Division. Educated at Windlesham House School, Grove House School, Tottenham, and the University of London, he was now a senior partner in the family firms of Thomas Barlow & Brothers, of Manchester and

→AN ADDRESS←

DELIVERED BY

VISCOUNT WEYMOUTH, M.P.

TO HIS CONSTITUENTS

AT THE

Mechanics' Hall, Frome,

ON

The 18th Day of November, 1887.

ANNOTATED AND REVISED.

The Frome Newspaper Printing and Publishing Company, Limited, 1, Church Street, Frome.

London, as well as Barlow and Co., of Calcutta, Shanghai, Singapore, and Kuala Lumpur which traded in commodities such as tea, coffee, and rubber.

The general election took place throughout the month of July and Frome recorded an 81.7% turnout of the 11,031 registered voters that now existed in the division. With 52.7% of the electorate's having put their mark next to Barlow's name (equating to 4,747 votes) against Thynne's 47.3% (4,260) it meant the former had secured victory with a majority of just 487.

It was enough though and saw the start of the long association with the Frome seat (with a brief period of respite – see below) that lasted well into the early part of the next century.

However, Thomas Thynne was not finished with the Frome Division and stood against Barlow again in 1895. This time it was Thynne who secured victory, but with an even further reduced majority of 383[3]. But fate was on Barlow's side and within the year he was MP for the Frome Division again. This came about due to the death of Thomas Thynne's father, the 4th Marquess of Bath, in April 1896. This meant Thomas was elevated to the peerage, taking his father's place in the House of Lords, and triggering a by-election. His younger brother, Alexander

Thynne, took his sibling's place to contest the seat, as the Conservative candidate, but was beaten by just 299 votes by Barlow[4].

The victorious Weymouth in 1895, outside the Frome and District Conservative Club, which stood at the top of Bath Street, opposite what is now The Cornerhouse (Author's Collection)

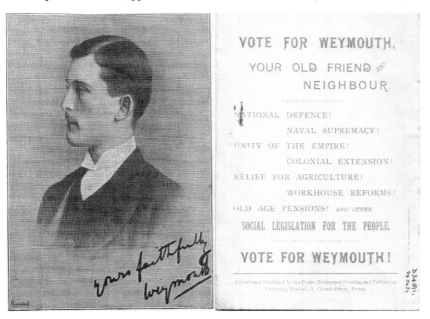

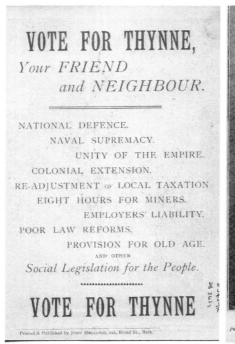

VOTE FOR THYNNE,

Your *FRIEND* and *NEIGHBOUR*.

NATIONAL DEFENCE.

NAVAL SUPREMACY.

UNITY OF THE EMPIRE.

COLONIAL EXTENSION.

RE-ADJUSTMENT of LOCAL TAXATION

EIGHT HOURS FOR MINERS.

EMPLOYERS' LIABILITY.

POOR LAW REFORMS.

PROVISION FOR OLD AGE.

AND OTHER

Social Legislation for the People.

VOTE FOR THYNNE

Printed & Published by JOHN MELLISH, 22a, Broad St., Bath.

LORD ALEXANDER THYNNE.

Printed and Published by THE MEISENBACH Co., LD., *Wolfington Road, West Norwood, London, S.E.*

Previous: Promotional material for Viscount Weymouth's electoral campaigns – probably 1895 – along with younger brother's similar one (above) for his unsuccessful 1896 by-election campaign. (Frome Museum)

Despite John Barlow's small majority, this victory would be the start on an unbroken twenty-two-year tenure as the Frome's MP, during which time he would successfully contest four general elections. The first of these was in the opening year of the new century. His Conservative opponent in the 1900 general election was Ellis Hume-Williams. Hume-Williams was a barrister, a King's Counsel (KC), and in October 1901 would be appointed Recorder of the Borough of Bury St Edmunds. He had attended Cambridge (Trinity Hall). In 1895 he had unsuccessfully stood for the seat of North Monmouthshire and would be so again in Frome[5]. Barlow's 5.066 votes put paid to his opponent's chances of victory, with a total of 4,708, increasing the winning candidate's majority by 59, to 358. By now, the electorate was 12,317 and just under 80% of them turned out to make their vote count.

FROME DIVISION.

ELECTION, 1896.

YOUR VOTE and INTEREST

ARE SOLICITED ON BEHALF OF

J. EMMOTT BARLOW, ESQ.,

THE LIBERAL CANDIDATE.

Printed and Published by Harvey & Woodland, Frome.

Promotional material for John Barlow's 1896 by-election campaign, in which he won the seat back from the Conservatives by defeating the outgoing MP's younger brother, Alexander Thynne (Frome Museum).

The next general election would be in 1906, and Barlow would have the first of three encounters in four years with the same opponent, scoring a hat-trick of victories. The unfortunate gentleman was Charles 'Chas' Talbot Foxcroft, who stood as the Conservative and Unionist candidate. Foxcroft was the son of Edward Talbot Day Foxcroft (1837–1911) – born Edward Talbot Day Jones and the owner of Hinton House at Hinton Charterhouse in Somerset – and wife Wilhelmina Colquhoun (née Robertson-Glasgow). He would inherit the estate on the death of his father.

Mr. CHAS. T. FOXCROFT.

The first electoral contest between Barlow and Foxcroft would see the Liberals nationwide win a landslide majority and Barlow himself increased his several fold, from 358 in the 1900 election to 1,745 in this one. But despite two further successful campaigns, both in 1910, this electoral win can be seen in hindsight as the peak of his political prowess. Never again would he enjoy such a large majority and it was downhill from here. But whatever downward slope his political career might be on, the following year saw Barlow created the 1st Baronet of Bradwall Hall in Sandbach in the County of Chester.

The result of the 1906 general election being declared at the Old Police Station in Christchurch Street West. The deputy returning officer, with results in hand, is R.P.H. Batten-Pooll. The candidates stand either side of him –Barlow to his right, Foxcroft to his left. Barlow wins with a majority of 1,745, the largest of his political career, although this will also be the peak of his political prowess. (Frome Museum)

1910 was a year of two elections, at either end of the calendar. The first, in January, saw Barlow's majority slip to 779, a decrease of about 1000, although there was a record turnout of nearly 90% of voters. In December, despite victory, Barlow's majority, slipped even further, by another couple of hundred votes. The double election year had come about due to the rejection of the People's Budget by the Conservative-dominated House of Lords. The first was called by the Liberal government to obtain a mandate for the budget, but after that resulted in a hung parliament, another had to be held in December.

The next general election was set for the end of 1915, and by July 1914 the candidates had been selected. With Foxcroft having seemingly given up the ghost[6], Barlow's opponent this time would be the Unionist Candidate H Barker-Hahlo.

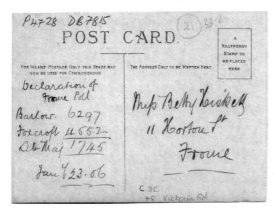

Promotional material relating to Charles Foxcroft's campaign (Frome Museum)

FROME DIVISION OF SOMERSET,

Parliamentary Election, 1910.

Probable Polling Day: FRIDAY, 28th JANUARY.

Your **VOTE** and **INTEREST**

are earnestly solicited on behalf of

MR. CHAS. T. FOXCROFT,

Conservative and Unionist Candidate.

A Policy of—More **Employment** for Britishers.
An adequate **Navy.**
Maintenance of the **Union with Ireland.**
Consolidation of the **Empire.**

Printed by F. C. Barber at the "Chronicle" Offices, 33, Westgate Street, Bath.
Published by Stanley C. Abbott, Chief Conservative Agent (Frome Division, 4, Walcot St., Bath.

Declaration of Poll at Frome, Jan. 29

The election of January 1910. This saw the second of three encounters between John Barlow and Charles Foxcroft, all of which were won by Barlow. This time his majority was 779, down around 1000 from 1906.

According to an article in the Somerset Standard[7] *'[Foxcroft's] place has been pluckily filled by Mr. H Barker-Hahlo, a man in the early prime of life and with tremendous fighting qualities. His energy and industry on behalf of the cause amaze all who come in contact with him. He is a resident in the division, at Camerton Court, which is in the heart of the Somerset coalfields, and since his adoption last spring as prospective Unionist candidate has visited practically every corner of the division, and is familiar with the requirements of the electorate. The working men in the constituency appreciate his strong personality and sterling, honest qualities. There is nothing vague about his views upon the political topics of the hour. His omnipresence is astonishing, and he is to be found taking part in every laudable work in the district, besides being a good all-round sportsman'.* Despite all these platitudes, Barker-Hahlo never got the chance to see what the electorate really thought of him through the ballot box, as with the start of the First World War in August 1914, the 1915 election was cancelled.

In retrospect, the war did not go well for John Barlow, and the seeds of what would be his post-war political defeat can be seen to have been sown throughout the conflict. Even in his personal life the war brought an immediate problem. His wife, Lady Barlow, who was attending a church conference in Germany at the time of Britain's declaration of war, found herself and her group briefly stranded in what was now a hostile and enemy country. Although faced with difficulties, Lady Barlow and her companions did finally manage to return to Frome, albeit without their luggage.

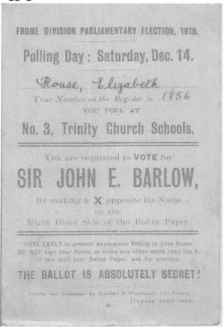

It was to be on more militaristic issues that Barlow's political career would falter. As revealed in my book, *Frome in the Great War* [8] *– 'The demise of the Derby Scheme ultimately led to the Military Service Act or conscription. The bill was approved in January – although controversially Frome MP Sir John Barlow, a Quaker and pacifist, voted against it – and came into effect two months later, on 2 March 1916. The Act required all single males of British nationality between the ages of eighteen and forty-one to undertake compulsory service in the armed forces. Within three months this was expanded to include all married men in that age group and by the end of the war, the upper age limit would stand at fifty.'* It also did not help that while too many of Frome's sons were being killed on the fields of France and Flanders, Barlow sent his own son to America, in the guise of education, for the war's duration.

When war came to an end in November 1918, an election was quickly called for the following month. The 1918 election, held on Saturday 14 December, would be the first election to have all voting nationwide take place on a single day. It was also the first election in which women (or at least those over 30 with access to property) could vote, as well as standing as candidates. With the escalation of what had now become the 'Irish Question', the knock-on effect of Home Rule for Ireland had been to split and weaken the Liberal Party. It is quite remarkable, when looking back, that from their landslide victory of 1906, they would effectively be a spent force within twenty years.

If the national party was having trouble of their own making, then so was Barlow in Frome. A new prospective Conservative candidate had been chosen to face Barlow and this was Percy Angier Hurd[9].

Hurd (pictured left) was a journalist but would become the first of four generations to serve as Conservative MPs. He was editor of *The Outlook*, a weekly magazine that had been published in London since 1898, a member of the executive committee of the Agricultural Relief of Allies Fund, and during the war had made several visits to the front lines on fact-finding missions. In 1918, he stood in Frome as a Coalition Conservative candidate and was in possession of the 'coalition coupon'[10]. This meant that he enjoyed the full support of the Liberal-Conservative Coalition government and as results would show, the majority of those with these so-called 'coupons' – this election would become known as the 'Coupon Election' – secured victory over those without; Barlow being one such candidate of the latter group.

Before the election could take place there were further boundary changes to those that had occurred back in 1885. The number of constituencies in Somerset was reduced from nine to seven and with it, Frome Division's boundaries were extended westwards to the fringes of Bristol, bringing in Midsomer Norton and the areas round Clutton, Chew Magna and Keynsham (previously in the Northern Division) along with a few other areas. Despite these changes, or possibly because of them, the Frome Division remained marginal, but had also became the second largest constituency in the country.

Along with the boundaries, there was also an expansion in the number of candidates. For the first time in over sixty years, there were more than just two candidates vying for the seat: this time there was four! Along with the Conservative Hurd and Liberal Barlow, Labour had put forward a candidate, as had the National Party.

Edward Gill, often known as Ted Gill, was a socialist activist who had been a coal miner. Although born in Herefordshire, he had moved with his family to Abertillery in Wales when he was ten years old. When the First World War began, he had initially opposed it, but quickly changed his mind and joined the 10th South Wales Borderers. Once at the front, his bravery earned him the Military Cross. He was badly wounded later and invalided out, with the rank of Captain. He then dedicated himself to the Labour Party, which was still less than twenty years old, and in the 1918 election became the first Labour candidate to stand for Frome.

What Sir John Barlow stands for.

A Peace of Justice,
A League of Nations,
Limitation of Armaments,
Abolition of Conscription,
Quick Return of Soldiers to Civil Life,
A Higher Minimum Standard of Life,
Justice to Ireland.
Maintenance of Free Trade,
Equal Opportunity in Education,
Drastic Land and Housing Programme,
Liberal Pensions for Soldiers and Dependents who have suffered through the War.

VOTE FOR BARLOW!

The final candidate for the Frome seat in the 1918 election was Lieutenant-Colonel Thomas Malcolm Harvey Kincaid-Smith. In 1894, Smith had been commissioned as a second lieutenant into the 9th Lancers. He was then promoted to lieutenant the following year and seconded for Colonial Office service in 1898. He had fought in the Second Boer War and was promoted to captain in 1903. Not long after, however, ill-health forced him onto half-pay and in 1908 he had resigned his commission. Before the latter event he had been elected Member of Parliament for Stratford-on-Avon in 1906, but in 1909, resigned his seat and left the Liberal Party to advocate compulsory military training.

After leaving the Liberals, he stood as an independent, supported by the National Service League, at the ensuing by-election, but was badly defeated. He was recalled into the regiment on the outbreak of World War I and had held several ranks, ending up as a temporary major. The National Party, who Kincaid-Smith stood as candidate for in 1918, was a short-lived British political party created in August 1917 as a right-wing split from the Conservative Party. When all the votes were counted, it was Hurd who had gained victory, securing a majority of 664. But if defeat for Barlow was bad enough, it was not even himself that the majority was over. It was Gill who had secured 10,454 votes to the Hurd's 11,118. 'How the mighty have fallen' could be applied to Barlow in this instance, as he came third with only 2,004 votes, a mere 8.4% of the total and nearly 45% down on his last pre-war victory. And so, after twenty-six years as Frome's Liberal Member of Parliament (albeit for that one year between 1895-6) along with a previously similar period of Liberal dominance in the seat before he stood (again, except for two years – 1874-76 – in which Conservatives held power) Frome would now reflect the nationwide trend: that of the demise of the Liberals as the main opposition party and the rise of Labour to take their place.

If Barlow could take any comfort, although it would not have been much, at least he did not come last. That 'honour' went to Kincaid-Smith and if his result was anything to go by, it was easy to see why the party he stood as candidate for did not last long. He secured only 258 votes, equating to a mere 1.1% of the total number cast.[11]

When the next general election was held in 1922, Frome Division returned to just two candidates vying for the seat – Hurd and Gill. Sadly, for Gill, the result was the same, although he achieved a respectable 14,311 to a winning total of 15,017 (a majority of 706); Gill's share of the vote equating to 48.8%. This would be Gill's last outing as candidate, as he died the following year and was replaced by Frederick Gould, who had been born in Midsomer Norton and was a trade unionist. Gould came from a mining family – his father had been one of the founders of the Somerset Miners' Association – with a strong Methodist background. He had left school at 12 to begin work as a stable boy.

Gould did not have long to wait to campaign for the seat, as an election was called in December 1923. Nationally, the Conservatives, now headed by Stanley Baldwin, won the most seats, but a combination of those secured by the Ramsay MacDonald led Labour Party – who now became its first Prime Minister – and H. H. Asquith's reunited Liberal Party produced a hung parliament. Frederick Gould was one of the seats won by Labour, enjoying a 2,596 majority over Percy Hurd and began what would be a 'ding-dong' battle that would last until the demise of the county constituency in 1950. Hurd's defeat was a major blow to the Frome Conservative and Unionist Association and a meeting was called to ensure the necessary steps were taken to *'strengthen our Organisation so as to be ready to meet the requirements of another Election and to be determined to reverse the present position.'*

With the chaotic political atmosphere that ensued after the 1923 election result, it meant the Frome Conservatives had the opportunity to 'reverse the present position' ten months later, in October 1924. Gould, less than a year into his victorious campaign, would now have to do it all again, but this time, against a new opponent, as Hurd had decided to stand elsewhere[12] .
Businessman Geoffrey Kelsall Peto – who would later become a director of Morgan Crucible Company – had been unsuccessful when he stood in the Lincolnshire constituency of Louth in

1923. However, in the 1924 election, held on Wednesday 29 October that year, he was able to achieve the Frome Conservatives' desire to 'reverse the position' and his 16,397 votes to Gould's 14,652 did just that.

D2590/1

FROME CONSERVATIVE AND UNIONIST ASSOCIATION.

Rowden House,

Frome.

IIth December 1923.

Dear Mr Sardley

    The result of the Election and the return to Parliament of Mr Gould as the Member for Frome has caused me to take a careful stock of the situation, and I feel sure that all Conservatives and all Constitutional Supporters will pause to think of the dire results that would follow a Labour Government. Now is the time for us to strengthen our Organisation so as to be ready to meet the requirements of another Election and to be determined to reverse the present position. It seems to me clear that the Local Organisation has not had the active co-operation from the influential members of the Town that it should have done. In order to obtain this and to obtain a real co-operation I am writing to invite you to attend a Conference of about fifty of our Party to be held at The George Hotel, Frome, on Monday next the I7th day of December, 1923, at 8 p.m. At this Conference I shall lay before you my views, and I hope that we shall obtain the views of many present as to the best method of proceeding. I trust that you will make a special point of attending if you possibly can as now is the time for us to move and to correlate our joint ideas in an endeavour to meet the position which has arisen.

Yours sincerely

Bennett Cruttwell

A letter written by Cruttwell announcing the meeting and declaring that the Conservatives need to 'reverse the position of the 1923 election.'

After the upheaval of the previous period – with three elections in as many years – things settled down and Peto enjoyed a five-year tenure as Frome's MP. He would not have to think about campaigning for the seat again until 1929, when an election was called for May. Things looked in his favour, as he faced two opponents – one Labour, one Liberal – with the possibility of them splitting the opposition vote, thus allowing him to retain his seat, being a likely outcome. In the end though, a 2,146 majority saw previous incumbent, Frederick Gould, retake the seat, with Peto coming second and the Liberal's candidate, Colin Stratton-Hallett, a poor third, with only 14.2% of the total vote.

In the 1931 election Gould defended his seat against yet another different political opponent[13], this time in the shape of Henry Frederick Thynne, aka Viscount Weymouth. Thynne was the second son of Thomas Thynne, who had been the town's MP back in the 1880s and 90s. He was educated at Harrow and Christ Church, Oxford and although the second son, became heir apparent to his father's estates and peerages after his elder brother, John, was killed in action in the First World War. In the 1920s the tabloid press had labelled him as one of the 'Bright Young Things'. If successful, he would become the third Thynne family member to represent Frome in the House of Commons.

In the end, Thynne's victory was all-conquering, resulting in a 7,110 majority over his rival. Out of a turnout of 42,606 voters, he had secured 58.3% of them, equating to 24,858 votes. Gould's 17,748 paled into insignificance and signalled what would be his swansong election in Frome.[14] If Labour's Frederick Gould was not there to contest the seat in the next election, when it took place in 1935, then neither was the victor. Deciding he wanted to concentrate on business interests, Thynne made it known he would not seek re-election and was ready to hand the reins to someone else.

LORD WEYMOUTH, M.P. for the Frome Division, with Lady Weymouth and Mrs. M. C. Tate, M.P. (right), the prospective candidate. Lord Weymouth will not seek re-election.

The candidate eventually chosen to take over from Thynne was Mavis Tate. She had been born on the island of St Helena in 1893 and baptised Maybird Constance Hogg. She could count as relatives the merchant and philanthropist Quintin Hogg, his son Douglas McGarel Hogg, who would serve twice as Lord Chancellor and later became Lord Hailsham, and his son, also called Quintin, who, like his father, served twice as Lord Chancellor, the second time during Margaret Thatcher's premiership. Mavis changed her name from Hogg to Gott, when she married an army Captain during the First World War, but after a divorce in 1924, changed it once again to Tate the following year. Her second husband was Henry Burton Tate, whose ancestors had merged with the Lyle family, to create the famous sugar company. She had entered the House of Commons in 1931, when she became MP for West Willesden, but with her husband's health a major factor, had later been looking for a more rural constituency. She had caused something of a shock when she had won at West Willesden and although Frome was currently Conservative, would have her hands full to secure victory once more. Her opponents – and there were two – were Kim Mackay for Labour and the Liberal Philip William Hopkins. Of the three, Tate was the only one with parliamentary experience.

Ronald William Gordon 'Kim' Mackay had been born in Australia and studied law and education at the University of Sydney. In 1932 he was a co-founder of the Australian Institute of Political Science, which argued for reform of the Australian Constitution. Encouraged by Labour MP Stafford Cripps to move to England, he had done so the previous year and began to practice law. Meanwhile, Liberal's hope for victory rested with Philip Hopkins. In April 1935, at his first public indoor appearance after being adopted as his party's prospective candidate, he had spoken of his hope that the Division would return a Liberal candidate, sooner rather than later, whenever the next election came. Unfortunately, for Hopkins, when the chance did come later that year, the 4177 electorate who voted for him was not even enough for the return of his deposit [15].

It was, as had been the case for the previous twelve years, a battle between blue and red. Mackay did well with 18,690 votes, but it was Mavis Tate who secured victory achieving a total of 19,864 votes, a majority just short of 1000. In winning, she became not only Frome's first female MP, but also that of Somerset, the county to which it belonged.[16] Adhering to her campaign promise, she rented a residence in the area – first at Nunney and then later, at Great Elm – and spent as much time here as Parliamentary duties would allow.

Despite a mutual admiration between population and politician which grew increasingly throughout her term, Tate intended to stand down at the next election (which was to be held in 1940)[17] and so a successor had to be chosen. The candidate chosen was Guy Dalrymple Fanshawe. Like Tate, he would face two opponents. Kim Mackay stood again for Labour, but the other was a candidate for the British Union. This was a far-right political party created by Oswald Mosley and indeed, Mosley came to Frome in 1938 to speak at the town's Temperance Hall[18] in support of his man, Charles Hewitt.

However, before the election could be held, the Second World War began and after Fanshawe went off to fight, Mavis Tate was persuaded to stay on. She therefore became Frome's wartime MP and for a time also stood in for the Bath MP, who had also been called up. Despite her dedication and work-rate, when the war came to an end and a general election was called for July 1945, she was swept aside by a Labour landslide. In a scene repeated up and down the whole country, wartime politicians were unceremoniously voted out and Labour came into power as people looked ahead to the peace they had won. In Frome's case this meant the new MP was Walter Farthing, with a majority of 5,507. The fifty-eight-year-old Labour politician, who had only just celebrated his birthday the day before the election, had been born in Bridgwater. He had become involved in the trade union movement and founded a trades council in the town. He was elected as the trades council's president in 1917 and served on Bridgwater Borough Council for the Labour Party from 1929. Although, like many before him, Farthing would only serve one term as Frome's MP (retiring in 1950) he nevertheless achieved the distinction of being its last, at least as far as this constitutional configuration was concerned. This was due to the fact in 1950, for the General Election that year, the Frome Division was abolished, and the town of Frome transferred to the Wells Division. But that, as they say, is a whole different story.

In the third and final part of this series, those MPs that represented Frome within the division of Wells and then, after 1983, the constituency of Somerton and Frome will be revealed.

FROME ELECTION RESULTS 1885-1950

1885
Liberal	**Lawrence James Baker**	**4,735**
Conservative	Thomas Thynne	3,972

1886
Conservative	**Thomas Thynne**	**4,348**
Liberal	Godfrey Samuelson	3,645

1892
Liberal	**John Barlow**	**4,747**
Conservative	Thomas Thynne	4,260

1895
Conservative	**Thomas Thynne**	**5,043**
Liberal	John Barlow	4,660

1896 (By Election)
Liberal	**John Barlow**	**5,062**
Conservative	Alexander Thynne	4,763

1900
Liberal	**John Barlow**	**5,066**
Conservative	Ellis Hume-Williams	4,708

1906
Liberal	**John Barlow**	**6,297**
Conservative	Charles Foxcroft	4,552

1910 (JAN)
Liberal	**John Barlow**	**6,248**
Conservative	Charles Foxcroft	5,469

1910 (DEC)
Liberal	**John Barlow**	**5,944**
Conservative	Charles Foxcroft	5,366

Boundary changes to the Frome Division effectively more than doubled the electorate.

1918
Unionist	**Percy Hurd**	**11,118**
Labour	Edward Gill	10,454
Liberal	John Barlow	2,004
National	Thomas Kincaid-Smith	258

1922

Unionist	Percy Hurd	15,017
Labour	Edward Gill	14,311

1923

Labour	Frederick Gould	15,902
Unionist	Percy Hurd	13,306

1924

Unionist	Geoffrey Peto	16,397
Labour	Frederick Gould	14,652

1929

Labour	Frederick Gould	18,524
Unionist	Geoffrey Peto	16,378
Liberal	Colin Stratton-Hallett	5,774

1931

Conservative	Henry Thynne	24,858
Labour	Frederick Gould	17,748

1935

Conservative	Mavis Tate	19,684
Labour	Kim Mackay	18,690
Liberal	Philip Hopkins	4,177

1940 (not held)

Conservative	Guy Dalrymple Fanshawe
Labour	Kim Mackay
British Union	Charles Hewitt

1945

Labour	Walter Farthing	29.735
Conservative	Mavis Tate	24,228

Notes

[1] It would not be until the 1918 general election that voting took place on a single day. Until then, it was spread over an extended period.

[2] The Government of Ireland Bill 1886 is more commonly known as the First Home Rule Bill, by which the government of the day sought to enact a law creating home rule within Ireland.

[3] Thomas Thynne secured 5,043 votes to John Barlow's 4,660.

[4] Alexander Thynne would later become MP for Bath, in 1910, but was killed on service in the First World War.

[5] Like several previous losing candidates, Hume-Williams would later enter the House of Commons through victory in a different constituency; in his case this was Bassetlaw in Nottinghamshire at the 1910 election.

[6] Charles Foxcroft, like so many before him, had to go elsewhere to find Parliamentary success, although this time it came about through a tragedy. Alexander Thynne, who had campaigned unsuccessfully himself at Frome in 1896, but became MP for Bath in 1910, was killed towards the end of the First World War. In the subsequent by-election in October 1918, Foxcroft finally entered the Houses of Commons. He held on to his seat in the December

general election and was also successful in 1922. He lost the 1923 election but regained it the following year and then remained the City's MP until his death in February 1929.

[7] Somerset Standard dated Friday 17 January 1913 p.7

[8] Frome in the Great War – Lassman, D (Pen & Sword 2016) p.97

[9] Percy Hurd was the grandfather of Douglas Hurd, who served in the governments of Margaret Thatcher and John Major, and held various ministerial positions, including Home Secretary and Secretary of State for Northern Ireland.

[10] The 1918 general election would become known as the 'coupon election.'

[11] With the increased boundaries in the division, the total number of registered voters was now 35,222. Out of these, 23,834 votes were the total number cast in the 1918 election, which was a 67.7% turnout.

[12] In the 1924 general election Percy Hurd won the Devizes seat from the Liberals, who had been successful there the year before, and would remain its MP until he retired from Parliament at the 1945 general election.

[13] Gould's previous opponent, Geoffrey Peto, successfully stood for the Bilston constituency in Wolverhampton. This was his last election, as he retired from Parliament at the 1935 one.

[14] Gould would also be defeated in his final election, in 1935, when unsuccessful in standing for Leicester East.

[15] In 1935, this required a candidate to secure at least 12.5% of the total vote - Hopkins' total equated to 9.8%

[16] At the time of writing – February 2023 – Mavis Tate was Frome's only female MP in the 191 years since the town elected its very first MP, back in 1832!

[17] The main reason given was the cost of running a campaign and her current financial situation.

[18] Oswald Mosley was due to speak in Frome in 1937 but had been arrested in Manchester the night before.

August 1931: Cabinet ministers of the 'National Government' at 10 Downing Street. Back row (left to right): C Lister, J Thomas, Rufus Isaacs, Neville Chamberlain and S Hoare (Viscount Templewood). Front row (left to right): P Snowdon, Stanley Baldwin, prime minister Ramsay MacDonald, H Samuel and Lord Stanley.

FROME DARTS CHAMPION

Dr Patrick Chaplin

In 2005 darts historian Dr Patrick Chaplin, prompted by *QI* compiler and author Mat Coward, wrote a letter to the *Somerset Standard* in which he posed a number of questions relating to a photograph of the darts team from the Red Lion at The Butts which had appeared in a previous issue.

Patrick contacted the *Standard* asking about the rather unusual dartboard shown in the photo and wanted to know more about the pub and the darts team. He also asked for information about other teams in the area in the 1920s, 30s and 40s and was particularly keen to know if Frome had produced a *News of the World* darts champion. Patrick was delighted by the response and wrote:

The Red Lion Darts Team 1929-30

'I was absolutely thrilled that so many people contacted me following the appearance of my letter in the *Standard*. Ron Doman recalled seeing the rather unusual dartboard when he was a lad and told me, 'The board has been gone for donkey's years.' When Ron was old enough to throw a dart in the local pub, he was playing on the dartboard made of wood (probably elm) with no treble ring, no outer bull (25) but with the same numbering and size as a standard clock board but, Ron revealed, 'The doubles were twice the size.'

'Twice the size' indicates to me that this was a home-made dartboard with the doubles being bigger so that games could be finished more quickly. With at least a half pint of beer going to the winner of each game you can see that the quicker the games were over, the more ale would be sold. It is not surprising then to learn that this type of dartboard was known as 'The Landlord's Board.'

Ron Doman was a keen dart player himself and played for 'one of the best teams around' from the 1940s, until 60s at the Castle Inn, Frome. In the 1970s he 'won everything' at the Cross Keys, Corsley including the *News of the World* house champion title two years running. Unfortunately, he was unable to make it to the venue for the next rounds - The Railway Hotel, Westbury - because he was 'snowed in' on both occasions.

Tony Austin contacted me and confirmed that the Red Lion used to be a 'hot - bed' of darts. He told me they had a very good team and when he played for them during the period 1969-1972 eight singles were played every Monday and four doubles matches on Wednesdays. The landlord at the time was Roy Hanney, now deceased and the Red Lion closed in 1982 and is now housing.

William Heydon of Frome
Courtesy of Ken Whatley

As regards the question of the *News of the World* Individual Darts Championship, both Ron Doman and Ken Whatley came up with the name WILLIAM HEYDON as the only dart player from Frome to make it to the national finals. Ron said that Bill used to play out of the Castle Inn, Frome and was 'a great dart player.' Bill's parents, Albert and Emily Heydon are recorded as landlords of the Red Lion between 1922 and 1939. Ken told me that Bill was a personal friend of his since leaving school in 1944 up until Bill's death in 1957. Ken remembers William as a very popular man and recalled that he and Bill played with Jim Pyke style brass darts but that 'we made our own canes and paper flights'. Ken added that, 'Bill made the best of his ailment.' Apparently, Bill suffered with chest problems for most of his life.

I wanted to know more about this great Somerset darter, and further research showed that in March 1949 the *Somerset Standard* reported that he had made it through to the *News of the World* national individual finals at the Empire Pool, Wembley having become the Western Division champion at the first attempt. (Bill had actually entered the previous season but ill health meant that he had to withdraw.) He had qualified for the divisional finals by becoming the North Somerset area champion and went to Exeter Civic Hall to play in the divisional final and in the quarter-finals beat W. Prentice, (George and Dragon, Bodmin). In the semi-finals he defeated C. Symonds, (Stoppford Arms, Stoke, Devon) and then, in the final, he dispatched the South Somerset area champion D.E.Thomas, (Conservative Club, Chard) two games to one. The *Standard* described Bill as, 'an all-round player' and hope that he would bring 'national honours to the town'.

The *News of the World* programme for the Grand Finals held in London on 9 April 1949 featured some biographical details of Frome's finest, it stated:

> WILLIAM HEYDON. House champion of the Castle Inn, Frome; area champion of North Somerset; divisional champion of the Western Counties. Aged 34, single and a sheet-metal worker. When he was a boy of fourteen Bill had a attack of paralysis which stopped him from taking any further part in strenuous athletics or outside sports. Fortunately, his father, now deceased, who kept the Red Lion at Frome taught him to play darts. Darts and his 74-year-old mother, (whom he hopes will be watching him tonight), have become his twin loves. Bill entered for the competition last year but had to withdraw due to a recurrence of his old trouble. So he has achieved the distinction of getting to Wembley virtually at the first attempt. Has won several competitions in the Frome district, but tonight is his first really big night. If he takes the cup back to Somerset it will be a triumph of pluck over adversity.'

The programme also featured a photograph of Bill, who lived in Bridge Street, being overwhelmed by his lady supporters from Frome, amongst whom I am certain would have been his beloved mother. Unfortunately, Bill not make it to the final being eliminated in an earlier round. The eventual winner was the London and Home Counties divisional champion Jackie Boyce. Later, in the 1957 season, by which time Bill was playing out of the Griffin, Frome was runner-up in the *News of the World* Somerset area finals. That was to be his last success as he died that same year at the age of only 42.

By reaching the grand finals of such a major darts competition in 1949, Bill Heydon had certainly made his mark in a competition which boasted total entries in excess of 250,000 nationwide. He had brought great pride to the darting community of Frome and the town in general.

Another reader, Joe Tate from Crockerton near Warminster, telephoned to tell me about Walter Clark from Horningsham who won a set of the *News of the World* silver darts in the 1930s at the Ship Hotel, Mere. In an autobiographical article published in the *Warminster Journal* in 1996 Walt looked back at the win and said that soon after he won the darts, 'I had them pinched from my overcoat at the Bath Arms, Horningsham whilst I was up the skittle alley.'

Joe also kindly provided me with a photograph of the Maiden Bradley darts team which won the Frome Merchant Navy Week's darts competition c.1941/42. The photograph is reproduced here together with the names of all the team members amongst them Walter Clark.

Back row: Ernie Peck; Robert Seal; William Clark; Roland Norman

Front Row: Walter Clark; Basil Leather

Patrick described the response to his questions in the paper as beyond his wildest expectations which enabled him to gain a snapshot of darts in Frome and surrounding area over three important decades in the history of the game - but one important fact eluded him - the date of the start of the Frome Darts League. He is still on the hunt for information and would love to know more about Bill Heydon and any other Frome-based darts player who made the Grand Final of the *News of the World* Individual Darts Championship between 1949 and 1997. Dr Chaplin can be contacted at patrick.chaplin@btinternet.com

§§§

The full history of the town's pubs can be found in the book, *Historic Inns of Frome* by Mick Davis and Valerie Pitt obtainable from Winstone's Bookshop or Frome Museum.

THE MYSTERY OF PRESCOTT'S HEAD

Mick Davis

One winter's day in November 1983 police sergeant and amateur archaeologist John Prescott was out indulging his hobby of poking about in other people's trenches and holes in the ground. On this occasion his enthusiasm took him to the Clink area of Frome where Prowtings the builders were in the process of constructing a new housing estate. John had been looking for traces of Frome's ancient past since at least the mid 70s with some interesting finds to his credit. On this occasion he was looking for evidence of the route taken by the Roman road that connected Bath to Poole, in his own words,

> The excavated base for a new road had just begun where I saw that it had cut through a section of a much earlier metalled minor road or track. I cleaned up the face cross-section of the track and observed that its construction had been made up out of a narrow layer of Forest Marble placed atop the original soil surface. The surface had a covering of 'pounded' Forest Marble. The measurements were: width approximately 11 feet, the centre was approximately 12 inches petering out to several inches at either side of a camber.

> I took the number of photographs and informed the archaeology department at Taunton. Mr Bob Cross BA the Somerset county archaeologist visited the site and I recollect he took a compass bearing along the rough route of the track. Several metres to the west of the old track and on the side of a small spring I had found and recovered a small stone head sculpted out of what appeared to be 'Bath' stone. This was in embedded in one of the mounds from the new road excavation material. The carving is that of an alleged local Roman god (Stephen Bird, Bath Museum) it now sits in the depths of the Castle Museum at Taunton, *I have yet to decide what should be done with it.* When Bob Cross visited the site he advised me to take it to the Roman Bath Museum, as they would probably want to examine it. Mr Bird of that museum did examine it and duly reported his findings. They then passed it on to the Castle Museum at Taunton.

> I had also recovered in the same mound of rubble and clay, what I assumed to be the 'fitting base' that the bust had rested upon. I would describe it as being quite heavy for it size, it has been formed from a smooth, dense mixture of a fired brick like clay of a deep reddish colour, it has no sharp corners in any part, all are well rounded and smooth. The shape is rather odd. At first glance it really looks like a broken off piece of modern brick that has been ground down into its present shape. One of its sides is slightly chamfered; 95% of the base is covered in a runny white lime cement mixture similar to that which still adhered to the base of the head. Instead of a fixing hole being central it is to one side and then there is only one half of the fixing hole, almost as if they should be another piece of matching brick that makes up the whole. A large part of the fixing hole contains the runny now hard and contents of the line mix with an indentation of where something had once been inserted. Measurements 11cm x 4.50cm x5cm. The fixing hole is at least 3.50cm in width. (and still in my possession).

HER 25712 Romano British head (SHC)

When the head was returned to Taunton after being assessed by Stephen Bird it was given the reference number HER 25721-map reference ST 793 488. Mr Bird published his report on the find in the Somerset Archaeological and Natural History Society's Journal Vol 129 for 1985 as follows,

The head is slightly smaller than life size, measuring 12cm wide, 15cm deep and a maximum height of 14cm. It appears to be that of a full- cheeked youth, possibly a woman, and is inclined upwards and turned slightly to the right. It is broken off above the eyes and the surviving features are very worn and, in places, damaged. The crown has been hollowed out to reveal the top of a dowel hole drilled up from the base. The shape of the hole's top indicates the use of a hollow conical drill. The hole, later plugged with plaster or stucco, suggests that the head originally belonged to a larger piece of sculpture.

The features of the face show the work of a skilled craftsman. The structure of the eyelids is faintly visible and a lightly drilled pupil in the left eye suggests a date in the second century AD or later. The centre of the right eye is, unfortunately scarred. The mouth is delicately fashioned with closed lips, but spoiled by an anomalous hole 9mm across, drilled in the right corner. The hole is too round to have held a flute or pipe, around which the lips would be contoured in the work of this competence, and the reason for it remains unknown. Most of the left ear is missing but the lower half of the right ear remains. As is common on much ancient sculpture the nose has been badly damaged and much of it is missing. The raised bridge, which curves smoothly down from the brow between the deeply recessed eye sockets, suggests a narrow but prominent nose.

The hollow crown, doubtless the reason for the break, may indicate the presence of a once substantial head-dress, perhaps a crown or helmet which would conceal the roughly tooled interior. The only surviving hair crosses the right ear and appears to have finished in a slight pad at the back of the neck, where the very simple shaping may indicate a plait or garland.

Despite the wear and damage, it is clear that the head has been masterfully fashioned in limestone, perhaps by provincial sculptor fully conversant with the principles of classical sculpture, and who may also have been accustomed to working in marble. The lack of detail on the areas of hair that remain suggests that it may have been only summarily rendered all over, and detail to hair and facial features was probably painted on to conceal the inferior quality of the stone which with a suitably smooth marble - like finish would be impossible.

Looking at the sculpture side - on it is immediately apparent that some of the damage to the

head is very recent and probably occurred as it was, scooped up by a mechanical digger during the roadworks. The break is shining white and the edges crisp and sharp in contrast to the rest of the head which is worn, rounded and discoloured. How much more of it survived the centuries we will never know.

A side view of the Romano British head (SHC)

It is most unfortunate that this important artefact now seems to have disappeared without trace. Extensive searches in Taunton have failed to find it and there are a couple of problems with John Prescott's account. In the first instance, there was not a County Archaeologist named Bob *Cross* working at Taunton, and Prescott has probably mistaken the name for Bob Croft, - but he was not working in Somerset until 1986. It is probable that his memory was deceiving him after so many decades and that it was another archaeologist that accompanied him on that occasion possibly Ian Burrow. Another problem is that he says in his account that he had *yet to decide what was to be done with it.* It is possible that if it ever was returned to Taunton he took it out again fairly soon after as he was perfectly entitled to do. It is also curious that he would retain the plain base of the sculpture having given up the main piece.

John Prescott died some years ago and attempts to contact any family have not proved fruitful so unless the head is found at the back of a broom cupboard in the depths of Taunton museum or appears in an auction room somewhere we are unlikely to determine its fate.

I am very grateful to Chris Webster of the Somerset Heritage Centre for his help and assistance in attempting to solve the problem and for the contemporary photographs. Before he left Frome for Grantham in Lincolnshire John Prescott deposited a typed account of his findings from 1980 until 2006 with Frome Museum from which this extract is taken.

The Frome Hoard from Witham Friary uncovered in 2010. Part of the growing evidence of a Roman presence in the Frome area

AN OPIUM EATER'S END

Natalie Owsley

Mr William Jeynes, one of the first medical officers of the new Frome Workhouse led a life that was arguably reflective of the disparity between public and private Victorian society. Publicly, Mr Jeynes was a responsible and virtuous man; a doctor and pillar of the community. Privately, he was troubled. The neglect of his patients and his duties often caused unnecessary suffering to those needing the most help.

How it began: A new welfare state and a brutal workhouse system

The Frome Workhouse opened in 1837-8 on the site now known as Ecos Court. Many workhouses, including Frome were increased in capacity or rebuilt during the introduction of new welfare legislation in the 1830s. Changes to the poor relief system in 1834 known as the New Poor Laws, sought to blame poverty on personal idleness. Previously, poor laws were ad hoc in their approach and interpreted differently by every parish – something which the government felt was open to manipulation. The new laws, controlled centrally by the government aimed to reduce the cost of looking after the poor, to reduce begging and most importantly, to combat laziness. To the rest of the world, the transactional workhouse system aimed to pave the way in effective welfare reform. A workhouse in each parish would provide shelter, health care, education and critically, a day's work in return for support. Workhouses were designed to physically segregate men, women and children but were also morally discriminative. Those who were suffering from mental health illnesses, venereal diseases and those with illegitimate children were especially at risk from violence, cruelty, and shame.

The Frome Workhouse was designed to house up to 400 *undeserving* men, women and children who were refused outdoor relief. Outdoor relief was support by way of money, medicine, food, or clothes and enabled *deserving* people to remain in their own homes. Those considered to be deserving were often thought to be morally good but unable to work due to illness, pregnancy or infirmity. Those deemed undeserving by the new legislation would only be offered help if they entered the workhouse; known as Indoor Relief. The undeserving poor were often unmarried mothers, the regularly unemployed, sex workers, those with a history of crime and known alcoholics. All were thought to be deliberately avoiding work. All decisions regarding relief (and thus a judgement of people's moral conduct) were undertaken by a group of men known as the Board of Guardians – consisting of local industrialists, solicitors, magistrates, and others who were keen to uphold their philanthropic Victorian duty.

The Workhouse Buildings Today (Natalie Owsley)

Research undertaken as part of a master's dissertation, concluded that the majority of people admitted to the Frome Workhouse between 1850 -1880 were young women with children and unemployed middle-aged men. Many suffered from long term debilitating illnesses, were illiterate and were trapped in a cycle of poverty. On the other hand, the older people of Frome were well cared for by their families along with private and religious charities. They were regular recipients of outdoor relief and considered to be deserving. The most vulnerable; young mothers, those with disabilities and men with a range of health problems were often subjected to the harshest scrutiny. Sadly, evidence also demonstrated that some women were so eager to avoid the scrutiny of the board that they actively avoided applying for relief, resulting in malnutrition, the loss of the lives of their children and in some cases, the loss of their own. The Board of Guardians and the medical officers had the power to subject those with the least agency and the least ability to help themselves, to the cruellest of conditions which often led to neglect, abuse, and the lowest quality of life.

Deciding to enter a workhouse was the very last, desperate resort for most people. All other avenues of help would have been exhausted by this point; the reliance upon kinship support, private charities and homelessness was a well-trodden cycle for many. Although a report in 1866 suggested that facilities at Frome were 'good', in reality (and hard to admit about our own history), conditions were woefully inadequate; child mortality rates were high, disease was rife and the threat of violence from other inmates and staff was a constant threat. The most common reason for entering a workhouse voluntarily was for medical care, even though entering the workhouse came with its own risks. Nurses within workhouses were often long-term female inmates with no training and no facilities. Although the rate of neonatal death was high, women chose to give birth in workhouses when the conditions at home (or on the streets) were even more perilous. Those involved in accidents or who had long-term health conditions would also enter the workhouse for intermittent treatment. Each parish had at least one medical officer who was a qualified doctor and would oversee the care and prescribe treatment to those receiving parish support. Medical officers were the vital connection between the pauper and the Board of Guardians, and their decisions were, for some, the difference between life and death.

The Suspicious Mr Jeynes

Mr William Jeynes assumed his position as the medical officer for Frome in 1850 shortly after he qualified. He was registered by both Royal College of Surgeons and the Licenced Society of Apothecaries. In 1849, he was living in Coleford on the outskirts of Frome with several other male lodgers. By 1851, after his accession to medical officer, we find him living in North Parade with two servants. Although a much-improved social position, parish medical officers were considered among the lower ranked physicians of the mid nineteenth century. The post was made available for tender by the Guardians but was often secured by those who would accept the lowest salary. Medical officers were also required to pay for their supplies and medications from their wages. Unfortunately, the potential manipulation of this part of the contract was something that attracted the more unscrupulous of society to the role.

Jeynes began his life in Newfoundland and Labrador. Born in 1825 to travelling missionaries in Canada, he was the only child of William and Sarah Jeynes. Mr Jeynes senior arrived in Canada as a teacher and although not officially a Reverend, was admitted to the Holy order of Deacons by the Lord Bishop of Newfoundland and Labrador. He served his tenure at St Thomas,' an Anglican church in St John's before returning to the UK where they became curates of Chantry Church. His parents remained curates throughout their lives, although they would move to London and serve at Christ Church in St George in the East, Tower Hamlets. William and Sarah lived a quiet life of service which perhaps initially appealed to a young William as being a doctor provided a certain level of social mobility along with regular work and a good wage.

It was, however, only a few short months before there were issues with the care provided by Mr Jeynes. By October 1850, it was brought to the attention of the Board that he was visiting patients but neglecting to record them in his reports. He subsequently provided an explanation for this which satisfied the Guardians. Three months later in January, Susan Parkinson's 13-year-old daughter Harriet was severely burned. When Jeynes visited the family, Mrs Parkinson claims that he refused to pay for her dressings and ointment and demanded she purchase them herself. She complained to the Board, and he was reminded that he was contracted to purchase any medications that he prescribed.

Inconsistencies continued to plague Mr Jeynes. On 19 July 1851, Mr Cruttwell (a member of the Board of Guardians), concluded that his conduct was 'by no means satisfactory' after he failed to visit the wife of a James Parfitt who later died. After reprimanding Jeynes, he once more reminded him of his duties and the conditions of his contract which was 'to provide medical relief to all sick paupers within the district, particularly when requested to do so'. Jeynes's first serious complaint came in April 1852, from the family of Harriett Hilliar. Details have been lost but were serious enough to be categorised as gross negligence and the board were 'bound to express in the strongest terms their disapprobation of the conduct of Mr Jeynes'. In July of the same year, he took some unofficial leave from his duties without first ensuring any satisfactory cover – a further misdemeanour.

The Master's Accommodation (Natalie Owsley)

By 1853, the relationship between Jeynes and the Board of Guardians was becoming understandably strained. In January, Jeynes reported that the diseased Mary Jacobs, (a poor cloth spinner) was suffering from, 'an eruption of the body'. A subsequent examination revealed that she was actually suffering from smallpox. He was once more asked to explain this discrepancy which, due to its contagious nature was a grave concern. At this point, Jeynes decided that he required further training in order 'to better himself' and thought it best to resign from his position. His resignation came with the request that the board provided him with a testimonial to secure his future employment. After the board refused his request, he finally resigned the following month without a reference.

In 1866, he married Mary Lambert, the daughter of a jeweller in Hereford and twenty years his junior. Jeyne's father had been born in St Owen, Hereford and perhaps there was a connection between the two families. Mary was just ten years old when her father died in 1849. Her mother was left to raise Mary, her older sister and younger brother. The prospect of a good marriage for her daughter would have been desirable as her marital home had passed to her sister-in-law after her husband's death. Little is known about the early years of the marriage but by 1871 they were living in separate properties in London. Mary was living at 2 Lower Teddington Hampton Wick and was described as a widow. William Jeynes was described as a surgeon and registered at the house of a blacksmith named Henry Barrett – he was, however, recorded as a servant and not as a visitor or boarder. Whilst census returns are often fraught with disparities, it is likely that most people felt a certain responsibility to be truthful in their answers. Certainly, most enumerators knew their communities well and had a good understanding of the relationships within homes and therefore it is likely there was a separation in their relationship at this point.

By 1881, the Jeynes had resumed cohabitation and were living in Vine House, Kingston Upon Thames. He was now described as a general practitioner. They were living with Mary's niece

Edith and several boarders including two servants in a house of multiple occupancy – life seemed more settled for them. However, by 1884, Jeynes had resigned as the medical officer for the Kingston Upon Thames Union. As in Frome, his tenure was plagued by complaints of inadequate care and neglect, and he left under the shadow of accused negligence.

An opium eater's end

By 1890, Jeynes was living in Safi, on the Western coast of Morocco and working for the British consul. Described as an oubliette for undesirables of the nineteenth century, Morocco and especially the western port towns like Safi, provided vital trade routes between Africa, the Mediterranean and Britain. There was a steady flow of exported ceramic goods along with trafficked drugs. Drug taking in Victorian society was widespread. There was little control over substances and cocaine, opiates, heroin and Laudanum were all readily available. Jeynes was forced to leave his employment in Morocco when he was discovered stealing opium. His tolerance was so high that he was able to consume four grains in one dose when ordinarily, just one grain would be fatal.

Safi, Morocco 1900

Returning to Britain in 1893, aged 67, he found cheap lodgings in a rundown apartment in Deptford and suffering from bronchitis which required treatment at the Greenwich Infirmary. It was here that he was discovered unconscious after taking a fatal overdose of morphine. The drugs had been provided for him by an unsuspecting official who believed the wallet Mr Jeynes requested, contained only the addresses of friends and family – to whom he wished to write. After his death, officials found enough morphine to kill 90 people in his belongings. Unable to save him, Jeynes died alone in a pauper's bed in the Greenwich Workhouse. His life having taken an ironic full circle.

In a patriarchal society that was obsessed with expansion and modernity and held virtuosity in high esteem, there was a juxtaposed appetite in Victorian society for drugs, illicit sex, and crime. As always, those with the least agency were unfairly and unjustifiably affected by those with the most power. The inability to break the cycle of poverty some found themselves in, meant they fell victim to men like Jeynes who were able to manipulate the system for personal gain. Jeynes was a trusted local official, addict, and potential drug dealer; a reflection of the double standards of Victorian Society which so often left those needing help open to the most abuse.

THE BLACK BOY, WALLBRIDGE

Mick Davis

There is certainly no shortage of strange names attached to the pubs of the British Isles from *The Crooked Fish, The World Turned Upside Down* to *The Bull & Mouth*. Multiple entries in the church rate books refer to various properties in Frome as '*near the Black Boy*' which indicates that it must have been a prominent landmark. The name alone is of interest and there are several possible etymologies, including references to chimney sweeps, miners and servants. The most likely origin is that it refers to King Charles II, nicknamed *The Black Boy* by his mother Queen Henrietta on account of his swarthy appearance - a dark complexion presumably acquired his from his Italian maternal grandmother Marie de Medici. During his flight after the disastrous Battle of Worcester wanted posters described Charles as a '*tall, black man*'. In other words, the *Black Boy* was another name for the King's Head and there are estimated to have been around 70 with that name in the country presumably celebrating the end of the Puritan regime. It would be an interesting exercise to see if the name could be traced back to before the restoration of 1660. The name was in the news recently when in a bizarre move surely at the cutting edge of silliness, the brewers, Greene King decided to rename three of their Black Boy pubs in case they were thought to be racist!

The Original Black Boy? King Charles II

The earliest reference to the *Black Boy* at Frome is the payment of church rates by Henry and Walter Merchant in 1679, some eighteen years after Charles II had been restored to the throne. The Merchants were still there in 1693 as tenants, the pub being part of the immense Longleat Estate holdings. In 1702 a lease was granted to Richard Rose, cordwainer, for the property *called or known by the name of the figure of The Black Boy*. In this lease Longleat retained their rights to the timber from all trees on the property and in addition, Rose had to plant three apple or pear trees and three oak, ash or elm trees each year. John Wayland took over the lease in 1710, and in 1732 he was paying 4d in the church rates for *Ye Blackboy*. Wayland remained there until 1733 when a lease was granted to John Young, who died in 1748. William Kellow, or possibly Kells, was in occupation in 1766, and seems to have been convicted for selling beer without the necessary license in 1785.

But where was it? The pub is clearly marked with its extensive orchard on a map by John Ladd of 1744 now held by the Longleat Estate and the building is shown as a 'house and garden' owned by John Meares on the Jeremiah Cruse map of 1813 plot no. 1222/3 The last known reference to the inn is in a document in Frome Museum which states, *Black Boy taken down by*

John Meares and dated 1834.[1] The site now lies roughly beneath the B & M store and the petrol station in the area leading to Frome railway station.

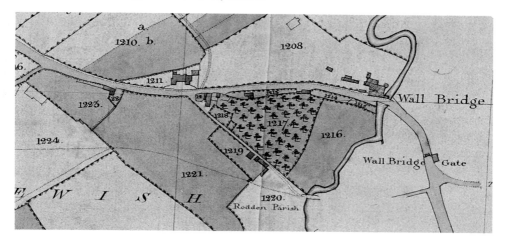

From the Jeremiah Cruse map of 1813 plot 1222 just above plot 1223

[1]1834 Little Hewish 17 acres lower end of Jacks Lane. Black Boy taken down by J Meares. Ground in use. D1117 Box 102 Frome Museum

§§§

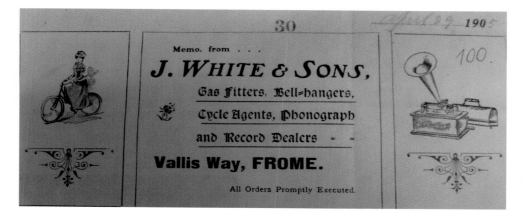

Trade Ad from 1905

DEEPEST SOMERSET

The third book in a series of tasty county reviews by Fanny Charles and Gay Pirrie-Weir, - and all for charity.

Authors Fanny Charles & Gay Pirrie- Weir

SOMERSET has become big news in the past decade or so. If you think of our county – and, apparently, these days a lot of people do – you probably picture truckles of traditional farmhouse Cheddar and flagons of cider (or better still, Somerset Cider Brandy), Lorna Doone's Exmoor, birdlife on the Somerset Levels, donkeys on the beach at Weston-super-Mare ... but there is so much more.

In the south east corner, Bruton, just a few miles from Frome, with a handful of uber-fashionable restaurants, is regularly depicted in the media as a Notting Hill-in-the-country rural idyll, with a host of celebrities, including fashion designer Stella McCartney, former Chancellor George Osborne, television presenter and property expert Sarah Beeny and actor and film star Benedict Cumberbatch – all 'living the dream.' Meanwhile a South African billionaire is reinventing not only beautiful Hadspen House and its gardens, but much of the surrounding farmland and countryside as The Newt, a new sort of theme park, which even boasts its own 'Roman' villa. Of course, Somerset is, much more complicated and interesting than the celebrity incomers and gentrification might suggest. Between Frome and Shepton Mallet, for example, are two of Europe's biggest quarries, one so large they say you can see it from the moon. A few miles north-west of Frome is Radstock, where a massive pit wheel and a few rather man-made looking hills recall the area's centuries of coal-mining.

Go west to the coast near Bridgwater and you can see Europe's biggest infrastructure project under construction – Hinkley Point C nuclear power station. It has brought employment and better training facilities as well as controversy.

Further west in the Brendon Hills you can find relics of the incline, the vertiginous railway that carried the iron ore from Exmoor down to Watchet and across the Bristol Channel, where its quality contributed to the manufacture of Bessemer steel. It is said that at weekends, the empty wagons carried a female cargo back up to the miners' camp, where they perhaps provided more entertainment than the strictures of the minister at the nearby Beulah Chapel!

Due north of Frome is Norton St Philip with its spectacular thirteenth century George Inn, said to be the country's oldest tavern, which saw action on both sides in the brutal Monmouth Rebellion. It was the headquarters for the Duke of Monmouth on his ill-fated quest to unseat the unloved Catholic King James II and later the setting for one of Judge Jeffrey's Bloody Assizes, ending with 12 local men executed as traitors.

More recently, as well as being a great pub with good food, the George is a popular location for period television and film dramas, including the famous seduction scene with Albert Finney in the 1963 film of Tom Jones, Pasolini's 1971 version of The Canterbury Tales, Merchant Ivory's 1993 Remains of the Day and a 1996 Moll Flanders.

With Long Sutton and Street, Frome was witness to the upheavals of the Quakers, Methodists and others who left their mark in simple, elegant buildings and a tradition of dissent that makes this county a far from 'safe seat' for any one political party. Frome's 'dissenting' sites include a Wesleyan chapel, a dissenters cemetery and Rook Lane Chapel, now home to an architects' practice and a multi-use arts centre.

For centuries an important centre of manufacturing and industry, Frome today is a creative hub with its unique Frome Independent market, Merlin Theatre and ECOS amphitheatre, Black Swan Arts, Memorial Theatre and one of the best arts festivals in the region. It is home to the composer Helen Ottaway, to ground breaking dance company Mark Bruce, and the most recent addition is Emma Rice's adventurous Wild Children theatre company.

Deepest Somerset, the latest book by well-known local journalists Gay Pirrie-Weir and Fanny Charles, explores the complex, millennia-old history of Somerset, and its rich tapestry of myths and saints, farming and food, wildlife, literature, dramatic hills and mysterious wetlands, Elizabethan manors and Perpendicular churches, and ancient carvings – from the glories of Wells Cathedral's West Front to the gleefully grotesque hunky punks around the church roofs at Langport, Curry Rivel and Isle Abbotts.

The book is a wide-ranging portrait of this county with an introduction by King Charles III – His Royal Highness, the Prince of Wales, as he then was – reflecting on the importance of the connection between people, farming, food and the landscape. Writing in 2020, he reflected on the quality of Somerset craftsmanship and the powerful connection between the people of the county and its landscape: "People need this connection because farming plays a profound cultural role. It is why it is called 'agri-culture' and why terms like 'agri-business' and 'agri-industry' are so misleading. ... We dwell within the landscape that feeds us and within the culture that is derived from maintaining its rhythms and natural cycle. Alas, modern approaches break that cycle, flattening it into the straight line of an industrial production process which severs us, not just from the source of our food, but from the sacred and cultural aspects of a community's precious sense of place."

Frome and its surrounding landscape embody this connection – within a radius of a few miles are some of the country's finest cheese-makers and cider-makers, and many of the new generation of craft and artisan food and drink producers, from brewers to chocolatiers.

The heritage of great local food and farming is celebrated in the Frome Cheese Show, the annual agricultural show held in September. Founded in the early 1860s, the show had various sites, including the former Singers Field, but is now based at West Woodlands, a few miles south of Frome. The success of the show and of the weekly Frome Market led directly to the building of a market hall in 1875. That building is now the Cheese & Grain, hosting a packed programme of local, national and international musical talent, from rock to folk to rap to classical.

The best-known cheeses are the traditional farmhouse Cheddars made by the Keens at Wincanton, Tom Calver at Westcombe, Jamie Montgomery at North Cadbury, Barbers at Ditcheat and the Trethowan brothers at Hewish. At Bagborough, near the Bath and West showground, White Lake makes award-winning goats, sheep's and cows' cheeses, including the distinctive ash-covered Tor named after the landmark which can be seen from the dairy. A former music industry executive, Marcus Fergusson left London with his family for a new life, making outstanding continental-style cheeses at Feltham's Farm near Wincanton. His best-known, both award-winning, are Renegade Monk and Rebel Nun.

A few years ago, apple orchards were being grubbed out and cider was a mass-produced shadow of the real thing. Now there are artisan and craft producers all over the county, led by Julian Temperley at Burrow Hill, the man who won the right to call his apple spirit Somerset Cider Brandy, a famous victory over the EU. The Burrow Hill success is reflected in the number of artisan cider producers across the county.

Newer products, but all with an ancient heritage, include Porlock Oysters, Somerset Charcuterie and Somerset Membrillo, produced at an ancient farm at Kingweston near Somerton.

If you are interested in the provenance of your food, you can't do better than visit a farm shop – Somerset has some of the region's best. They include the Kimber family's Kimbers Farm Shop, close to Wincanton Racecourse, the Bartlett family's picturesque and tiny Red Barn Farm Shop at Mudford (a must for the best fresh asparagus you can buy, in season), Teals at North Cadbury, serving locals as well as travellers on the busy A303 , Pitney Farm Shop off the Somerton to Langport road, and Whiterow Farm Shop, off the Frome bypass near Beckington.

Run by Heather and Steve Tucker – and doubtless well-known to many Frome residents – Whiterow is a destination shopping experience. There is a popular cafe, a fish and chip shop (open in the afternoon!), vintage shop, gift shop, florists and the farm shop itself, which specialises in home-grown and reared produce, from excellent meat to the freshest possible vegetables, including "petits posies" (baby kale sprouts, also known as kalettes), and the best fresh fish counter in a wide area.

Dig into a taste of Somerset

Finally, here is a taste of Somerset, from Deepest Somerset's own chef, Philippa Davis – pictured in a casserole from the world-famous John Leach Pottery at Muchelney.

Pot roast Somerset lamb shoulder with cider, Renegade Monk cheese and crostini with Somerset membrillo.

Somerset produces exceptional lamb, hogget and mutton. In this recipe I have slow-cooked it in one of the county's most famous products, cider, and served it with a crostini topped with Renegade Monk cheese and Somerset membrillo.

Renegade Monk
This unique washed rind, soft blue cheese was created in 2017 at Feltham's Farm. Within months it was winning awards and in 2020 was crowned Best British Cheese at the Virtual Cheese Awards. Made from pasteurised organic cow's milk, washed in ale and aged for about four weeks it's a funky, lively cheese with an underlying creaminess. www.felthamsfarm.com

Somerset membrillo
Trish Maunder produces award winning membrillo and bullace butter in her farmhouse kitchen. Quince, often regarded as a forgotten fruit, looks similar to a pear but its hard, tart flesh can only be eaten once cooked, when it becomes soft, golden and deeply fragrant. Membrillo is the Spanish name for quince cheese, a hard jelly with a rich sweet fruity flavour. Bullaces are wild plums and butter is a traditional fruit paste. www.somersetmembrillo.co.uk

Somerset Lamb

Philippa Davis's casserole of Somerset lamb with Renegade Monk cheese and Somerset membrillo, served in a pottery casserole from the famous John Leach Pottery at Muchelney. (Hugh McNish Porter.)

Visit almost any of the county's superb farm shops or butchers and you should be able to buy lamb that has been grazed in Somerset. If you can find it, the salt marsh lamb is rather special but due to the diverse fauna and flora in the luscious pastures and meadows throughout, all meat has an impressively full rich flavour.

Serves 6

1 large red onion, peeled and sliced
1 fennel, sliced into 8 wedges
4 sticks celery, cut into 2 cm lengths
6 fresh bay leaves
1.2 kilo rolled Somerset boned lamb shoulder
500ml dry cider

Crostini
12 slices of baguette
1 Renegade Monk cheese
12 teaspoons of membrillo

Pre heat the oven to 160C fan

Put the onion, fennel, celery and bay in a casserole dish with a lid, and place the lamb on top. Pour over 450ml of the cider and season well. Tuck a piece of baking parchment over the top and cover with the lid.

Bake in the oven for around 4 hours or until the lamb is tender. You will want to baste the lamb a couple of times during cooking.

Once cooked add the rest of the cider (this will help add some fresh fruity notes to the sauce) and check the seasoning.

For the crostini, pre-heat the grill to high. Lightly toast both sides of the baguette slices. Place a slice of cheese on each piece of toast then grill until hot and bubbling. Remove from the grill and top with a spoonful of membrillo. Serve the hot lamb in slices with the crostini and some blanched greens. This dish works well with mashed potato or smashed celeriac.

*Deepest Somerse*t is the third in the series of Deepest Books by Fanny Charles and Gay Pirrie-Weir, following *Deepest Dorset* (2016) and *Deepest Wiltshir*e (2019). Funded by a charitable foundation, the books raise funds for charities within the three counties. To date, more than £100,000 has been given to the beneficiaries, which include the Community Foundations for Dorset, Wiltshire and Somerset, Dorset & Somerset Air Ambulance and Wiltshire Ambulance, Dorset's Weldmar Hospice, the Children's Hospice South West in Somerset, the military charity SSAFA's Wiltshire branch, and the Somerset Farming Community Network.

* Deepest Somerset is published by Deepest Books, price £25; for more information or to order a book, visit www.deepestbooks.co.uk or email info@deepestbooks.co.uk

LULLINGTON IN THE EARLY 19th CENTURY

as told to Revd. WA Duckworth in 1895

These reminiscences were found in the Somerset Record Office[i] and were recorded by Rev. Duckworth who visited Benjamin Grant, retired farmer and one of the oldest inhabitants of the village having been born there in 1810. In 1891 he was living with his daughter in Spring Gardens. More a collection of jottings than an essay it has some interesting information.

Thatched cottage next to Widow Dymott which I pulled down used to be Lullington school, a private school, 6d a head for each child. If three in a family, three could go to school for 1/- a week. Mrs Pearse (school mistress) took in washing from Frome. Husband, hedger, ditcher and mower worked by piece because on Mondays he collected the clothes from Frome and on Fridays he took the clean clothes to Frome.

A watercolour by one of the Duckworth family c 1860 (Frome Museum)

Old Hall's House, (now the old post office).
The place before it was built was where the refuse of the parish used to run. Two thatched cottages used to stand near the refuse rubbish heap, the property was in Chancery, no repairs, cottages fell down.[ii] Old Hall, a tea traveller, built his house out of the ruins of the two cottages and occupied it when my father bought O.L.[iii] Duckworth senior questioned Hall about his title

and told him that he might remain there undisturbed for his life. I (WA Duckworth), bought the cottage and garden in 1878 subject to Hall's life occupation rent free. He died in 1895.[iv]

Black Death in Lullington.

Gypsy recommended peeled and put under the bed as a cure. It cured one case and a labourer who ate one of these onions which had been thrown on the refuse heap died eight hours afterwards. Sir Thomas Champneys gave old Benjamin Grant's father £2 for half a sack of Prince & Beauty potatoes rough potatoes with a pink eye. Benjamin's father had paid a guinea and a half for one sack of them at Warminster. At that time a 4lb loaf cost 11.5d. The labourer was not living but starving in old days, but now he has every advantage. Wages are now 14/- or 15/- instead of 9/- or 10/- and food and clothing a little more than half the price, but they are not so well off now as they spend it in pride.

Lullington Village c.1905

Benjamin has six pillions, (man and wife riding on one horse), going out of Lullington on a Wednesday morning to market. At that time, they were taxed £5 a year for a trap, £2 for a horse and £1 for the man to look after the horse. If you went down to Lullington you would not have found a piano then, Sir Benjamin's father was a former tax collector used to bring the dues home.

Present postman's grandfather, (Francis) lived at Whatcombe for many years, more than 50. Old Francis had three daughters who worked at lace with bobbins and made 15 Guineas for one veil, what they call Honiton lace. They dressed very smart in church, slippers and sandals, they made stockings in various shades of colours, with small holes so that one could see the flesh of their legs. One of these, the youngest, is Mrs Ashby now living as a matron at Keyford Asylum, a widow, her husband drank, very bad and brought her low. Are used to live at

Brokeover.[v] The labouring class much improved but the middle-class want something done for them.

Mr Wood Wright of Park Hill house, Frome keeps show dogs and has lived at Darwen[vi] on County Council. He has been two years at Parkhill with Mr Williams.[vii]

Advice. Always grind your own pepper, chemists add salt to keep it when it is ground. Go to bed at nine pm. Eat watercress when you first wake up in the morning and drink linseed tea last thing at night. At Collins's[viii] watercress is always grown and carried to the mansion by Sir Thomas Champneys. Watercress is a fine thing for young ladies!

The village at the turn of the century

---

[1] SRO DD/DU 151

[2] This would indicate that it was owned by Sir Thomas Swymmer Champneys, master of Orchardleigh who ran up enormous debts and whose story is told in, *A Surfeit of Magnificence, The Trials and Tribulations of Sir Thomas Champneys of Orchardleigh*, by Mick Davis, Hob Nob Press 2021

[3] Orchardleigh, Duckworth is now writing about his father and himself, the family tended to spell the estate's name as Orchard Leigh

[4] *Kelly's Directory of Somerset* for 1894 refers to John Hall as a baker & grocer

[5] A farm at Spring Gardens, Frome

[6] A property owned by the Duckworths in Lancashire

[7] Rev. W Williams rector of Lullington & Orchardleigh once headmaster at Frome grammar school.

[8] Longhouse Farm at Orchardleigh

THE FROME SOCIETY

FOR LOCAL STUDY

The Frome Society was founded in October 1958 when a group of local people got together to preserve the history of Frome in all its forms from buildings, manuscripts, traditions, natural environment and folklore at a time when much was being lost or demolished and the beauty of the town was under serious threat.

In 1966 the Society established the Frome Museum with which it still works closely. Volunteers curate artefacts, organise exhibitions, and maintain an extensive research library of local history open to researchers by appointment throughout the year. Many aspects of the town's history have been researched here leading to the publication of a large number of books and pamphlets mainly funded by the Society. We have also been instrumental in the erection of a number of plaques around the town marking historic events or important residents. There is an extensive programme of town walks, summer outings and lectures throughout the year as well as the opportunity to meet like minded people and exchange ideas at our annual lunch and quiz.

Our website is fsls.org.uk and our email is info@fsls.org.uk

As part of its work the Frome Society operates in close association with the Frome & District Civic Society founded in 1970 which has a very important role to play in the town, focusing on planning, the built environment and sustainability in general. They can be contacted on mail@fromecivic.co.uk

If you are interested in architecture, archaeology, geology, conservation, historical research or social history, then you will be interested in the Society and its aims. We have been involved in the production and publication of well over 100, books and monographs. Many are out of print but are slowly being scanned and made available on our website as downloadable PDFs. We are continuing to look for new authors and welcome anyone with ideas for new topics.

Other benefits of membership include a free copy of the annual *Yearbook* a fully illustrated journal of over 140 pages full of information and articles about the town and surrounding area. A twice-yearly newssheet, *Contact* contains details of the lecture programmes, outings and news of forthcoming activities as well as reports from the Civic Society. This is usually emailed to members.

Annual Subscription rates

Single Membership: £15
Joint Membership: £20
Life Membership Single: £150
Life Membership Joint: £200
please contact membership@fsls.org.uk

BANK DETAILS   Frome Society. Barclays Bank sort code 20-05-06   account. 90037966

There is a large selection of over 90 books and publications on Frome, its history and outlying villages downloadable as a PDF please contact publications@fsls.org.uk Orders by post are fine and postage is charged extra at cost. Please contact the publications address for a list of free out of print publications available in PDF format.

Publications on are also available in person from: -

Frome Museum, 1 North Parade Frome   BA11 1AT info@frome-heritage-museum.org   01373 454 611

Winstone's Bookshop, 9 Cheap Street, Frome, winstonebooks3@gmail.com   01373 473 111